Believest Thou This?

Ethel L. Johnson

BELIEVEST THOU THIS?

Cover Design: June Swad

Published by G Publishing, LLC
P. O. Box 24374
Detroit, MI 48224

Printed in the United States of America

ISBN: 0-9776780-1-6

Library of Congress Control Number: 2005937915

~DEDICATION~

This book is dedicated to the loving memory of my son, Isaac Tremaine Brown – October 20, 1976 to July 23, 2003, and my granddaughter, Iszakel Tremaine Brown – August 29, 2003 to September 1, 2003.

Isaac was murdered in cold blood at the age of 30. He was a warm, compassionate person with a wonderful sense of humor. He always took up for the underdog and made friends everywhere he went. He was a wonderful son, grandson, brother, father, uncle, nephew, cousin and friend to all parties concerned. I cannot begin to tell you how many loved ones he left behind but his soul mate and his five children will definitely feel his lost presence.

Iszakel died of kidney failure and other things that contribute to the death of extremely premature babies. Iszakel was born a twin and her sister will grow up knowing she shared her mother's womb with another beautiful soul. During the three days that she lived, we loved her very much. Isaac and Iszakel will be kept alive in our memories for as long as we are living.

Isaac Tremaine and Iszakel Tremaine, here's to you. God loves you and so do we!

~ACKNOWLEDGMENTS~

I would like to give special thanks to my mentor and friend, Minister Jo' Ann Mims, whom if it had not been for her believing in me, this book would not have been published at this time. I thank her for blessing me financially and for having faith in me. Thank God for you Jo'. You encouraged me when my belief in myself was waning.

I would also like to thank someone special to me, Michael G. Steward, Sr. Michael has been a key figure in helping me get this book to the publisher. Not only has he blessed me financially; he has been a special friend and a real encouragement to me to walk by faith and not by sight. I thank God that he sent you to my life.

I also give special thanks to Cheryl Riley. Cheryl has been a real encouragement and a friend to me. Not only has Cheryl been a financial blessing to me, she showed me the rainbow to remind me that God has not forgotten his promise to mankind. Thank you Cheryl. God put us in each other's paths and I thank Him.

Last but not least, I thank my son, Speedy Lamar and my daughters Karen and Melanie whom I love deeply. Thanks kids for believing in Mama and for always being there when I need you.

~FORWARD~

I met Sister Ethel Johnson at Ambassadors for Christ Church, Pastors Glenn R. and Karin A. Plummer. After reading Sister Johnson's book, it really opened my eyes to how you can be born today and die tomorrow. Trust me, you have to be saved, delivered and filled with the Holy Ghost in order to write a powerful book such as this. It took the Holy Spirit to write this book.

Sister Johnson talks about how her son was murdered in cold blood. It takes a saved person, because it is unbelievable that an unsaved woman or man could write of this type of pain and deep sorrow. I could feel her pain as I read the book. Her only son and her two daughters are still carrying their pain. This is a book you just could not put down until you finished. Besides, she lost her Twin A grandbaby too soon after the death of her son. Twin B is still living and healthy. Thank God.

If you have lost a loved one who was murdered, then this book is a deliverer from God.

Minister Jo' Ann Mims

~INTRODUCTION~

Everyone believes in something or someone. Some people believe babies are delivered by storks or are born in cabbage patches. At least they did when I was a kid.

What about God? There are some people who believe in a Supreme Being that created the world but only feel it is a spirit that really has no real bearing on our lives.

Still, there are others who believe there was an explosion (the "Big Bang Theory") in space and planets were formed. As a result of the explosion, some form of life began in the sea and ultimately developed into human life form. This type of belief would certainly contrast with Creation, which is what I believe in.

I am willing to bet that when Noah told the people that it would rain so much the earth would be flooded, they did not believe him either. They probably thought to themselves that Noah was crazy or on wine because it would be no way possible for a God to destroy all life. Even still, I am one who truly believes that the people had never seen water (rain) come out of the sky and they laughed.

But God opened the floodgates of heaven and the rain came down, non-stop. After about the third day of this, I would imagine the people started to think that just maybe Noah might be right and not so crazy after all. Yet, stubbornness can make us hold on to our beliefs even though different evidence is presented to us right before our very eyes.

Now it is the 21st century and more parents are burying their children than ever before. Children are killing children and innocent children are being gunned down as a result of drive-bys. I always thought that children should grow up and bury their parents of old age. What do you do when your heart is broken by tragedy or loss? Who do you turn to? How is it possible to ever again lead a normal life? My story is one that many people, somewhere in this world, go through every day. For instance, today is Tuesday, September 06, 2005 and I have been watching the tragic events of Hurricane Katrina that devastated parts of Mississippi and Louisiana. I have cried for the people of New Orleans as their town lay under water. This is the city where the Mardi Gras is held; where sex, nudity and robberies are prevalent. Would anyone have thought that God would have allowed so many to die? Is there a price for sin and disobedience? *"For the wages of sin is death; but the gift of God is eternal life through Jesus Christ our Lord."* Romans 6:23

What or who did the people of Biloxi or New Orleans believe in? As, I consider all the heartache and pain that I have suffered within the past couple of years, it has forced me to examine closely just what did I believe. Hopefully, reading my story will help you or lead you to examine just what, if anything, do you believe in? Nevertheless, whatever we believe in, we tend to put a lot of faith and effort into it. Let's face it; a lot of people are looking for a quick fix to solve their problems or to minister to their needs. There are all kinds of face-lifts, tummy tucks and energy pick-me-ups, self-motivation tapes, etc.

We are never really prepared for a tragedy in our lives. I just hope that something I say here in these pages will minister to your heart and help you gain strength to go through your season. Solomon said, "To every thing there is a season, and a time to every purpose under the heaven."

In the end though, after you have read "Believest Thou This?" I hope you are convinced that JESUS is the only way to the truth and the life; "I am the way, the truth, and the life: no man cometh unto the Father, but by me." John 14:6. Even if your interest is peaked enough to seek Him for yourself, I will have been a faithful servant.

Everything that I wrote in this book is true to the best of my knowledge. The names have been changed to protect the identities of the innocent.

Jesus loves you and so do I!

Ethel L. Johnson

CHAPTER 1} LIVING MY LIFE

~Growing up Baptist~

I presume that I have always believed in God or at least in a supreme being. I mean there always seemed to be awareness in me of good and evil. I had a problem with doing erroneous or wicked things without feeling bad or remorseful about what I had done. As a child, I went to church every Sunday. I grew up under the influence of the Baptist religion and most people I knew did or were doing things on the side; like drinking alcohol, smoking cigarettes or having unmarried sexual relationships. It was as though everyone thought that because they were doing things in secret that God could not see the things they were doing. They were going out on Saturday nights to dance with the music blasting and pulsating through their bodies. Then they would get up on Sunday morning with a slight headache or upset stomach. With the taste of liquor lingering at the back of the throat, they attended church, ushering, singing in the choir or just sitting in the congregation. Occasionally, the accidental burp would escape and the people standing closest to you would know your secret. I know because I was one of them who had secrets.

I carried that attitude and frame of mind into adulthood. My philosophy was that as long as I was not hurting anyone it was okay to drink a little liquor, smoke cigarettes or both. It was also acceptable to have a boyfriend, as long as you really loved one another. After all, everybody else was doing it and whose business was it anyway? I went to church sporadically. I would join, attend faithfully for a while, and then would wander away becoming what I heard was a "backslider." I just felt it was better to backslide than to be a hypocrite. I thought God respected me more by being honest and not sitting in church knowing full well that I had no intentions of not doing those things I thought made me feel good. I enjoyed drinking, smoking cigarettes, going out to nightclubs and having boyfriends in between husbands. I have been married twice. I did not have a clue that it was not mandatory to have a man. Therefore, I tried to keep one in my life.

Was God not eternal? Then he would be there when I was ready for Him. Even though, throughout my life when things would go wrong, I would pray to God and I feel He heard me. I even believe that He came to my rescue on more than just one occasion. However, that did not change the fact that the way I saw it – "seeing is believing and I could not see Him." After all, I was decent, wasn't I? I mean, I was not stealing or hurting anyone except maybe myself.

There was even an era in my earlier years when I was both angry and afraid of God. I thought He had something against me. He let my mother be murdered when I was 12 years old. I had no sisters or brothers that I knew of or had ever met. He let my fiancé be killed in Viet Nam. I was in my junior year of high school and we were going to get married after I graduated. Then, He allowed me get pregnant when I was in my last year of high school. I begged Him to give me another chance and take the baby back. I mean I was already in a foster home, close to graduating with no husband. Who needs a baby? Then when I was 22 years old, He let the only mother I knew and loved die. She was really my foster mother (the first one I had, not the second one). How could this God say He loved me when He broke my heart over and over again? Therefore, I thought I had better not love anyone else or God would take him or her away from me.

Thankfully, I outgrew that train of thought. So, I went on with my life the way I thought I should live it. After all, you can turn the TV on and hear someone saying how you should live your life for yourself, and if no one likes it, oh well. It was all about I am woman, hear me roar!

~I Got Me, Who Needs God?~

I never depended on God much and I only knew that Jesus was His son and he died on the cross for us to be saved. Boy did I have some questions.

Saved from what, I was not sure. I had pretty much made my mind up to believe that if I went to hell, so what. I would make the devil sorry he ever met me. I was a mean mamma jamma. My kids used to call me "Mafia Momma."

It was not that I was akin to Al Capone or Gotti but I could give a convincing bluff with my sharp tongue. *"Even so the tongue is a little member and boasts great things. Behold how great a matter a little fire kindles. And the tongue is a fire, a world of iniquity: So is the tongue among our members that it defiles the whole body, and sets on fire the course of nature and it is set on fire of hell: For every kind of beasts, and of birds, and of serpents and of things in the sea, is tamed and has been tamed of mankind. But the tongue can no man tame; it is an unruly evil, full of deadly poison."* James 3:5-8 Yes, some would say I had a mouth on me and I protected my family by whatever means was necessary.

Thank God, there were never any extreme measures that had to be taken. Well there was the one incident when a friend of mine held Pete over his head and threatened to throw him down. What didn't we hit that guy with that day. Pete was about eleven years old and the guy was at least 6'9." That was a long way down for a little guy like Pete. Lanie was about seven, and when the guy started to kick at our door and then our window, we decided to protect ourselves. I did not have a telephone, so I could not call the police. However, after we hit him and stuck him with whatever we could find, he became less of a threat and more a concern. Fortunately, the guy was okay, physically anyway.

• • •

Nevertheless, it sure was something about that gospel music. I loved it and with all my meanness and big bad ideas, "The Ten Commandments" and "The Greatest Story Ever Told" were amongst my favorite movies. When my children were old enough to understand, I read the Bible to them. I even bought them their own set of biblical books that included stories like "Noah and the Ark," "Moses," "Jonah and the Whale," "Daniel and the Lions Den," along with other favorites from the Bible. I took them to church in their earlier years although I did not press them to go to church, as they got older. My thinking was that as long as they were not killing, robbing or stealing, they were okay.

CHAPTER 2} THE CHANGE

~Bad Luck, Disrespect and Then Some!~

As the years rolled by, I went through my difficulties, trials and tribulations, heartaches and pains, misery and strife as well as my highest points in life. Yet, I felt that something was missing. I knew that there just had to be more to life than what I was experiencing. I was going through a period of what I deemed as "bad luck." I had lost my job, my apartment and found myself living with one or more of my adult children. It seemed to me as though this was developing into an unfavorable pattern. What mother wants to have to go live with her children? I tried to find a job but kept coming up empty. I found it questionable that with my profound computer and office experience why I had not been hired. I had even gained experience in property leasing. Working in an office servicing apartment complexes affords quite a bit of knowledge to put under your belt. I learned how to multi-task, collect, total and prepare rental payments for bank deposit. I also learned how to prepare court papers such as "eviction" notices, order office supplies, as well as other various office duties.

There are many facets in running the office. Nevertheless, I kept being presented with closed doors and obstacle after obstacle. So I drew unemployment compensation from the last couple of jobs I had worked. I had a place to stay, some income coming in and a steady boyfriend. So why was my life feeling consequently empty. I kept feeling as though I was about to explode. I was unhappy and discontented with just getting by in life financially, socially and even in matters of the heart.

I had not given much thought to the fact that something was changing inside of me. Certain activities were starting to get under my skin and not in a positive way; like watching my daughters, Kay and Lanie drinking alcohol and smoking weed all the time, even though I was drinking and I also smoked cigarettes. You know the saying "do as I say, not as I do," okay? I hated the smell of weed and it appeared as though it was all over the house lately. The living room had two or three people sitting on the couch watching the big screen TV and the smell of weed just wafted right on up to my room.

I stayed in my room day after day. Thank God, I had my computer because that helped to ground me. Sometimes when I had to go to the kitchen, I had to walk over or around a pair of legs on my way. My daughters Kay and Lanie were adults and had children of their own. Nevertheless, it started to bother me that each one of them had a man sleeping with them every night in our house and they were not their husbands. The stench of disrespect just started to sink in deeper and deeper. They did not try to hide much of anything;

and, the music, the language, the men, the drugs along with the alcohol started to pinch along my nerves.

My oldest daughter Kay moved out but the stage was set then and things were not improving. I also had Lanie's children to cope with. For everything they needed, they came to me. I love my grandchildren and wanted to care for them but when you have raised four children of your own, have at least 16 grandchildren altogether, the thought of rearing any more children was a little farfetched. Lanie, especially, took it for granted that as long as I was home, which was often, that it was my responsibility to take care of the children. Many days I found myself thinking that I should disappear somewhere, anywhere just to get away from everyone else's problems and troubles.

My two sons, Mack and Pete were at this time, stable and I was not overly concerned about their lives. My oldest son, Mack was living with his common law wife of 14 years. Gina, who is the mother of four of his five children, was his soul mate. They had transportation to come back and forth to visit and things appeared to be okay for them. Mack would often tell me to buckle down on my youngest daughter, Lanie and not let her worry me. He said I should learn how to tell her "no." They hung out together a lot and Mack felt that, although he would look out for her when she was with him, he did not approve of Lanie leaving her children with me all the time. Mack was a peacemaker though. So, he could have just been trying to keep peace between us. He loved both his sisters and in spite of the fact that Lanie stayed gone a lot, I was at least glad, she was at her brother Mack's house the majority of the time.

Pete had left Detroit and went south. When he first went down there, he became involved in selling drugs and drinking alcohol a lot. He was down there being the typical thug and I started to worry about him. I remember he called me one evening and while we were talking, someone interrupted him in the middle of our conversation. Upon asking him what was going on, he replied that his business was booming. I told him he needed to stop that mess and to be careful before he got into some sort of trouble. Pete called me periodically to check on us and to let us know he was okay. One night I received a phone call from him and he said, "guess what? I go to church now." My first thought was he meant he just went to church on Sundays like most people out of habit. Then Pete started to tell me that he reads his Bible and studies and that he was "saved." He informed me that he gave up worldly pleasures to follow Jesus Christ.

I was very happy to hear that Pete had decided to give his life to Christ. Even though I was not sure what it truly meant to be saved, I knew it was better than him being on the streets selling drugs. During one conversation we had, Pete said to me, "Momma you need to come on back to the Lord, let Him change your life too." Even while I held my favorite drink in my hand (which was Irish Crème Liquor) and as I slowly sipped it, I knew that he was right. "Yeah, you're right, I will," I told him. Pete said he was sending us all messages that he had received from the Lord and we would get them right before Christmas time. Each one of us was to read our own by ourselves because it was specifically for us individually.

~I Need An Angel!~

During the time Pete was in the south trying to live for Jesus and win souls, the devil tried to destroy him. People in the town did not understand Pete's type of faith and in his zeal to serve the Lord; he came across too stern and harsh with people. He felt everyone should repent and live for the Lord. He was like John the Baptist preaching in the wilderness. Therefore, powers of darkness started to work against Pete. People started to lie on him and even tried to get him locked up in jail. I was very worried and upset and began to talk with Lanie about preparations to go south, pick him up, and bring him back to Detroit. Things began to work themselves out for him though. Pete had God and His son, Jesus on his side. Even I, in my sin, knew that.

However, for me things were not getting better and that sense of being shut up in prison got worse. I stayed in my room much too often. But that is where I felt safe and the smells and sounds of the outside world did not affect me much. My second husband and I have been separated for almost as long as we have been married. That was almost ten years ago. Since this book is not so much about my life as it is a particular time in my life, I will leave out many details. Since my separation from my husband, I have had a boyfriend here and there. As I said earlier, I thought it was the normal thing to do.

I had a male friend that I was fond of but deep down I knew he was not the "one" that I was meant to be with. Reggie was nice and had a great sense of humor but he also liked to drink alcohol and smoke weed. In fact, he loved to smoke weed. I wore blinders and tried not to look at what was the truth of our relationship. Reggie was some years younger than I was, and his ideas about what was important in life was so different from mine. I remember that he had a daughter, who in the two years or so that we had known each other, I had yet to meet. I use to ask Reggie to bring her over to play with my grandchildren who were close in age to her, but he always made excuses. One being, that she was not use to any other woman being around him except her mom. Mind you now, that he was supposed to have ended this relationship with his daughter's mother for at least a year prior to our getting together. That was what he had related to me.

I wonder how many of us refuse to look at the truth in a relationship and see it for what it really is. It occurred to me that perhaps Reggie was ashamed that I was older than he was or that he only wanted to keep me in his bedroom for his sexual desires. All we ever did was go to his place, drink alcohol, fry chicken (his favorite dish) watch movies or listen to music and then go to bed. In view of the fact that most weekends consist of at least two days, "go figure." However, like many women, in the back of my mind, I thought, at least I have a man.

The day came when the oppression in my life was more than I could bear. My daughter Lanie and I had previously had an argument and it almost led to us fighting. Lanie has a gift for being disrespectful with that "in your face" attitude. She is good at pushing your "set it off" buttons when she cannot or does not get her way in a situation. At any rate whatever we argued about, it was enough for me to close my door and wedge a knife in it to keep anyone from coming into the room. The doorjamb was broken on the door and it did not close properly; that is why I would wedge a knife in it. I began to cry from frustration and talk to God. I told Him that I could not take it anymore and please send someone, one of His angels to help me. I felt like my daughters were literally trying to kill me. It was not long after that, Pete called and said he was coming back to Detroit. I did not know it right away but God had heard my prayers and His angel was on the way to rescue me from the demons of hell that were manifesting themselves in my daughters!

In the meantime, after my argument with Lanie, I left home, went to Reggie's house, and spent a few days with him. I knew there was a change coming because there was no excitement anymore in going over there. I was getting irritated with Reggie borrowing money from me. He started to act cheap and petty. I mean, he did not buy cigarettes but he wanted to smoke mine. In the beginning, he would buy me a pack and then smoke a few. Then he wanted beer or liquor but did not have the money this time around, so can you pay, and I will reimburse you. After awhile, this type of behavior starts to irritate you and you feel as though you are being taken advantage of because you are trying to be nice or helpful. Since Reggie was working, I believed him when he said he would pay me back. I guess it was just an irritation that he had to borrow in the first place.

I was indeed happy to see my son, Pete arrive from Arkansas. Before he got there, I had begun reading my Bible and started a prayer life. When I saw Pete, he looked so different. He was so clean and polished and the Holy Ghost resided in him and gave him a magnificent aura. The demons recognized that he was a mighty man of God and they began to take flight. He began to clean the area in and around our house. He made friends with the neighborhood teens and restored a basketball court across the street from the house for them to play ball. You should have seen the court. The court was covered completely with tall grass, weeds, sticks, dead tree limbs, glass, and other debris. When he started to clear the area, a few of the teens pitched in along with his nieces and nephew. Before long, the area was clean with a portable basketball rim and a few benches he found for seating. As he played ball with them, he also planted the seed of Jesus Christ, the Righteous, into their spirit. He would also let them hear his gospel rap which showed them that rap was not confined to hip-hop.

Pete, the kids, and I would sing songs and praise the Lord in the living room. Most of the time, the unsaved parties would stay gone because the spirit of the Lord was moving all over the house. Sometimes, when Kay and Lanie would have company, Pete would go and sit under them and just smile and listen to their conversations. It seemed as though they were always waiting and watching for him to slip up and make a mistake or get in the flesh. One day, he and Lanie were having a big argument and even got physical with each other. It reminded me of the old Pete and I asked Jesus, if indeed, he sent Pete to help me. He assured me that He had, because my spirit agreed with Pete's. Seeing as how no person is perfect, Jesus told me He was still working on Pete also. He was being renewed and restructured to fit into God's perfect plan. I was to exercise patience and have faith. I was beginning to feel whole again because I knew that God indeed, had sent Pete to help me and to strengthen and encourage me in my walk with Christ Jesus. We would study together sometimes and he helped to answer some questions I had as I began my spiritual walk. I had been saved I guess years ago but this time I was truly delivered from out of the world.

~Total Commitment and Faith!~

Many things were different this time around for me as far as my walk with the Lord was concerned. This time I was delivered from various strong holds on my life. I quit drinking, smoking, cussing, and yes, even fornication. I began to develop a relationship with Jesus that I did not have in the past. I tried to seek His face often by praying, fasting, reading the Bible, biblical references, watching gospel programs, visiting religious websites, and affiliating with other Christian Saints of God. I felt so filled up and I use to go in the closet, close the door, pray, worship, and praise the Lord.

One day while I was praising God, I felt all warm inside and light as a feather. My tongue began to move rapidly and I began to utter strange sounds. I started to cry and could not stop and I then realized I was filled with the Holy Ghost and speaking in tongue. What a feeling! When I finally emerged from the closet, it was as though something had been deposited into my spirit because things began to make better sense to me. I had a calm inside that was not there before. I joined church, went to Bible study, joined the Praise and Worship team, and truly tried to live for Christ the way He asks us to in His word.

Just how do you know when to use or exercise your faith? Going back a little to just before, I stopped smoking. I use to pray and ask the Lord to please take away the taste of cigarettes from my mouth. I especially did not want to smoke and call myself a saint. Not only that, smoking was affecting my health. I coughed a lot and sometimes had difficulty breathing. Therefore, I really, really wanted to quit. One Sunday, before I joined the Praise and Worship team, I was sitting in the congregation listening to the announcements. One part of the bulletin being read really sunk into my spirit and I felt an awakening in my soul. "It is not up to God to take away our bad habits but rather it is up to us to give them to Him." Yes, yes that is it. I immediately knew what to do.

When I left church, I think I had a little less than half a pack of cigarettes left. I made up my mind, started to pray, and told Jesus that I knew I would finish the pack but that after that I was giving the bad habit over to Him. When I finished the pack, I said "now Jesus it is in your hands." I told Him I never wanted to smoke again. That was over two years ago. It feels so good to be free from the bonds of tobacco, nicotine, and buying cigarettes. I have saved over $1,800 a year since not buying at least a pack a day at almost $5 a pack. Whenever an urge to smoke would enter my mind, I would call on the name Jesus for strength and the urge would go away just as quickly as it came. I had faith that Jesus would keep me from wanting a cigarette and He was there for me all the way. Blessed be the name Jesus.

As far as drinking alcohol, it was never really a habit for me but rather something I liked doing. Fortunately, it was easy to leave the liquor alone. Meanwhile, I was not anticipating the next meeting with Reggie. He could be a little opinionated and I really did not feel like debating with him about my newfound spirituality. It was Valentine's Day weekend when I went over to his house. We did our normal routine. In addition, he bought me a gift; the glass with the candy and a little white bear inside along with a card, which he conveniently forgot to sign. That was nice but one day I hope to mean more to my man than $10. God will make sure that I am his queen and he will be my king when we meet.

~No Sex, See Ya!~

Consequently, I mentioned to Reggie that I was going to give my life to Jesus and he remarked rather matter of fact, fine just as long as I did not withhold the sex. How typical of some male egos. Obviously, he was not aware of "thou shall not commit fornication, lasciviousness or uncleanness." He felt that it was not fair to him that I should serve Jesus and not administer to his needs. However, I already had my mind made up.

When I later told him that we would no longer be intimate, he could not believe it. He would say that he understood nevertheless he kept trying to get me to come over to his house. The Holy Spirit had already told me not to go over there because my inner man was not strong enough to resist the wiles of the devil when he released his demon of lust. Therefore, I told Reggie I felt that we should not be alone anymore just yet. I did not have to worry about it because he stopped calling or coming around. Where was the love?

I guess people will say anything until they are actually confronted with the reality of a situation. The gloves come off, the lights go on, and the ugly truth just jumps out at you. Love, if it is real, bears all things.

CHAPTER 3} GOD LOVES ME

~Sandy!~

I continued to worship and praise Jesus. I grew spiritually as I tried to serve him in spirit and in truth. I knew that I had gone to a higher level than where I started. When I would open my mouth to sing, my voice was strong and clear. I could feel that someone was being ministered to through my singing. It really was the Holy Spirit singing but using my voice. I even did some evangelistic ministry. I could just feel God moving in my life. I remember the first sermon I gave. It was called "If you love me, you will follow my commandments." Pete surprised me when he told me he had the tape from that sermon. I wondered what had happened to it.

I still did not have a job but the Lord supplied all my needs. He loaded me with benefits daily just like He said in his word. During the day, I would go out on the porch and stare at the clouds. It was as though I knew Jesus was up there above the clouds somewhere and that he was watching me. I could just feel his warmth all over me. Going out watching the clouds, reading my Bible and just communing with the Lord became one of my favorite pastimes.

I would take some of my grandchildren to church with me. We rode with BreAnn's paternal grandmother, Sandy. I called her twice grandmother because her son had a child by my daughter and her daughter had a child by my son. Not only was she a twice grandmother, but she was also a dear friend of mine. It was as if the Lord put us together because she came to our rescue on many of occasions. The type of friendship Sandy displayed was different for me because she was sincere in her motives when she offered her help. She would give the children and me money to put in church or buy us food and she never wanted repayment. Sandy would say that the Lord wanted her to do his or that for us and therefore she was doing as her Father in Heaven had instructed her to do.

I remember one day she wanted me to come and go somewhere with her. I thought we were going on an errand. Instead, she took me to pick out a washing machine, which she paid for and had delivered. Sandy said she wanted us to be able to wash the kids clothes without having to haul bags off to the laundry. How many of us have friends who would buy us something and not want anything back; especially something of any value? I was learning that saints of God were different from ordinary people of the world, including relatives.

The church I attended was a full gospel, non-denomination temple. I learned a lot attending Bible classes, Sunday school classes, and morning worship services. I enjoyed and looked forward to participating in, as well as leading the praise and worship services. I felt so anointed and there were other anointed leaders as well. There was one sister, Jessica, who was tall, graceful and had a rich jazzy voice. Jessica was different from most people because she knew who she was in Christ Jesus, and did not let anybody hold her spirit back. I admired her character and gained inspiration from her. She was also a gifted poet and I pray that God has blessed Jessica richly in her endeavors to get her work published. I hope to see her again some day so we can share our spiritual experiences and gain strength from each other's faith walks.

~She Could Have Died!~

Another incident boosted my faith up a few notches. I was sitting at my computer either playing a game or surfing on the Internet. My eight-year old granddaughter, BreAnn, was playing behind me. She was so energetic. BreAnn was always climbing up something, flipping, running, jumping, and a variety of other activities. This particular day, she had an ace bandage that I had for a little over a year. I remember the reason I had gotten the bandage in the first place. It was on my birthday, which is in July. We were having a little party at my son Mack's flat. They were barbecuing chicken and steaks for the occasion. I had fun playing and dancing with my grandchildren. However, as the night wore on, I had a few too many drinks. In the front yard of the building was a very large oak tree. The bottom of the tree was thick and gnarled roots spread out around it. The roots had protruded above the ground and were very slippery. I was headed to the curb to speak to someone in a car or something. I probably was getting ready to start an argument by putting my two cents into someone else's business. Anyway, as I headed across the yard, I slid on the roots of the tree. My feet went right out from under me and I landed on my back bumping my head a little, as I hit the ground. Mack carried me into the house and deposited me on the couch. Everyone was so concerned that I had hurt myself. Fortunately, I had only sprained my ankle and my niece wrapped it with an ace bandage.

Now here it is a little over a year and I have given my life to Jesus Christ. Anyway, BreAnn had the bandage playing with it. She tied one end to the handle on the top drawer of the Chester Drawers and the other end around her little neck. When I first turned in my seat and saw her doing that, I told her to stop it and to not play like that because she could hurt herself. I turned back to the computer assuming that she had done as I had instructed her. It was perhaps one or two minutes later that I heard a thump and I turned to see BreAnn again with the bandage around her neck. At first glance, I thought she was playing. But taking a second look, I noticed that her eyes were big, and her fair skin was reddening. BreAnn had slipped and lost her footing. She was sort of thrashing about because she could not stand up straight. Oh Jesus! I sprang out of the chair, grabbed BreAnn, stood her on her feet, and quickly unwrapped the bandage from around her neck. She was a little disoriented and frightened but was otherwise okay. I began to thank and praise God for saving her even in her disobedience.

Isn't that how it is though with all of us? God constantly saves us although we are so disobedient. I thanked and praised Him for allowing me to be in the same room with her. Otherwise, I might not have heard her when she hit the floor and it could have turned into a tragedy. "For the eyes of the Lord are over the righteous…" I explained to BreAnn the price we sometimes pay for disobedience all the while hugging her. I knew that an angel had been there in the room with us because the thump was soft and normally I would have ignored it thinking that it was just one of the kids playing.

CHAPTER 4} TRIALS, TRIBULATIONS AND DEEP SORROW

~Job, I Feel You!~

FAITH – that is one powerful word. *"Now faith is the substance of things hoped for, the evidence of things not seen."* Paul wrote that to the Hebrews 11:1. It means that you believe Jesus is who He says He is and that He can and will do what He said He would do. Some of the things He has already prepared and has ready for us to be released when we reach that place in our walk with Him. When we reach that place in our faith walk; when we run this race with patience; we have to look to Jesus because He alone is the author and finisher of our fate. Keep the faith. So how do you know if and when you have faith?

I was not feeling my best. I had some sort of eye irritation and I had gone to the altar for prayer. Soon after the irritation began to go away but in its place were hives all over my body. I thought maybe I was allergic to something but could think of nothing.

Anyway, I went into prayer and soon after the bumps started to fade. However, in their place were the unpleasant hemorrhoids. I am thinking what or who am I, Job, or somebody. Nevertheless, I kept praying that Jesus, by His stripes would heal me. See I truly believe that He was ever present and could hear all I said or thought. Soon after, the affliction went away.

As I sat on the porch one day shortly afterwards, I remember thanking the Lord for healing all of my ailments. I spoke to Satan clearly feeling victorious. I let him know that in spite of everything he threw my way; the Lord took care of it and made it for my good. I remarked to him that I felt like Job and asked if he planned to kill one of my children next. Why did I say that you ask? Only God in Heaven knows the answer to that question. Perhaps it was a prophetic thought.

• • •

It was July 20, 2003, Kay's boyfriend Tré's birthday. My birthday had passed six days before. My four children would usually get together and gift me or do something pleasant. Before Pete and I became saved from the conditions of the world, we all used to party together on birthdays. I would drink and dance right along beside them. That is why I feel compelled to pray for their salvation as well as my own. This year, though, there would be no celebration, only gifts and well wishing. It was something very different about this birthday. I could not have known that this would be the first of many birthdays that would never be the same.

Mack's car had broken down and he was not able to come over to visit me on my birthday. Our phone service was off so he was not even able to call me. I knew he would be coming over soon because he loved me and I loved him too. I loved all four of my children, however, this particular son just made sure that I knew he loved me by the little things he would do. He would come over, give me a hug or a kiss on the cheek, and immediately start to massage my shoulders. He always said I was too tense and needed to stop worrying about so much. That song by Bobby McFerrin, "Don't Worry, Be Happy" was one of his favorite songs. When he came over on July 20, he hugged and kissed me and wished me a happy belated birthday. He had brought me a gift and he, Gina, and I talked for a little while. He apologized for not being able to stay long because he was searching for Tré to celebrate his birthday with him. I told him it was okay and that I was glad his car was fixed so he could visit again. I had missed him and I was glad to see his car pull up.

Mack and Gina hugged me again and said their good-byes. They left out and got into their car. However, something compelled me to run outside after Mack. There was a real urgency inside of me and I knew I had to tell him something. I ran to the rail of the front porch and called out his name. "Mack, Mack," I called with a type of desperation. He answered and leaned over Gina so that I could see his face. "Yeah Ma," he said. "I love you. Don't be such a stranger" I said. "I love you too Ma. I won't be a stranger. I'll be over probably tomorrow or definitely the next day to see you," Mack told me smiling.

Gina had told me that Mack was having a fit because he had not seen me in a while and could not come over for my birthday. Then they pulled off and I watched Mack and Gina turn into the driveway across the street, come out the other end, and drive away toward Kay's house. I never, ever, in this lifetime would have imagined that would be the last time I would see my loving son, Mack's face. Is that why I watched until they were out of sight? Then I reluctantly went back into the house. What was that heaviness that came over me?

~If I Could Turn Back The Hands Of Time!~

It was Tuesday, July 22, 2003. I got up and started my day. It was a strange day and I remember feeling very weird. I made myself a cup of coffee, got my Bible, and went out on the front porch. I do this every morning except when I go job hunting. However, something did not feel right this morning. I tried leaning back in the chair and watching the clouds as I usually do. Yet, I could not concentrate for some reason and I felt very restless. Eventually, I gave up and came back into the house. I later wound up just going back to bed feeling so, so depressed and irritated. I could not put my finger on what was bothering me. Pete later came in from work or somewhere around 3:00 or 4:00 p.m. I was still lying around. I remember feeling irritated with Pete also, for what there was just no explanation.

At around 5:45 p.m., the kids came up to tell me that Sandy was outside and wanted to know were we going to Bible class and Praise rehearsal. She could not call because the phone service was still off. At first, I started not to go, but I thought that perhaps I would feel better if I went and got my praise on. Not only that, I did not want her having to come all the way to my house for nothing. Ultimately, I got up and went.

I do not remember the subject at Bible class or what we practiced in Praise rehearsal. I do remember the church giving us boxes full of food and goodies because when I got back to the house, Sandy blew the horn for Pete to come out. He came out and helped bring the boxes into the house. After Pete brought the boxes in the house and sat them on the table, he sat back down on the couch strumming his guitar. Usually Pete would have been in the boxes before he sat them down. It was as though he was waiting for something or someone.

I said good night to Sandy, came in the house, and started to unpack the boxes of food. Pete did not even bother to look in the boxes, which was truly unusual. He loved to cook and to eat. The time had to be close to 8:45 p.m. There was a knock at the door, and right here, forgive me, but things get a little cloudy. As I was putting the food away, I thought I heard Pete say, "I know you didn't say my brother just got shot and killed, I know you didn't just say that." I saw Pete kind of fall to his knees and bounce back up. From that point, things got even cloudier. I remember running to the front room and Pete holding me telling me he was sorry. I recall just calling on the Lord Jesus inside my head and thinking this is a mistake because God would not let this happen. The young man at the door had this sad, helpless look on his face and he also was saying how sorry he was. Why was everyone saying they were sorry? After all, I just knew this all was a big mistake. Surely, they had the wrong person. Pete ran out the door and down the street to use the phone of the young man who came bearing the dreaded news. I was left standing there with this sinking, aching feeling inside of me. I started to pace back and forth. I could not think straight and I could hardly breathe. "Please God, please do not let this be true. Lord, please, have mercy." I kept praying over and over again. Yet, there still seemed as though something was holding the dreaded thought at bay, that my precious son, Mack was dead. My granddaughter BreAnn told me later that I was crying so hard, my face looked like it was flooding. She said she was asking me what was wrong and I told her to leave me alone because I could not talk. I love BreAnn. I am sure she was comforting me as much as she could for an eight year old.

• • •

Now I can only relate to you the parts that I remember with any kind of clarity. I have heard that it is good therapy to talk about a tragedy and get your feelings out in the open. However, I also believe Jesus put a damper on some parts of my memory so that they would not be so painful. In time, as my healing progresses, I am sure the memories will return in their proper perspective.

• • •

I do not know how long it was before Pete came back to the house. I remember him, the kids and I waiting on the front porch for Kay to come and pick us up. Pete had learned from the phone call that Lanie and Mack were together when the devil ran him down and pumped multiple gunshots into his body. Yet, a part of me refused to register that word "dead." I just knew that when I got over there to Mack's house, it would be a lie and that he might be hurt but still alive.

Everyone was so silent when we got in the van. Tré was driving and Kay was sitting in the seat quietly beside him. We all seemed to be holding our breath. If we conversed about anything, it is a total blank for me. Ambulances, police cars, news vans, and people were congregating all in front of Mack's house. I jumped from the van and went to find my daughter, Lanie. When I saw her, I took one look at her face and all my hope drained from my body. I do not recall all that happened at this point. One minute I was holding Lanie and we were crying. I remember seeing Pete, Sr., and I think Pete, Jr., talking with the news reporter. I do recall ripping the buttons from the blouse I wore as I tore it from my body, while falling to my knees screaming and calling to God, "why"? As someone lifted me to carry me in the house, I remember hearing crying, screaming, and bits and pieces of the story being told. I do not even know when, how or why I went back outside. It appeared to me as though I was outside of my body watching myself go through some difficult motions.

~"Mack Needs Me!"~

I do not know what happened to the hours but Sandy was there in her car and I remember telling her that I had to get to the morgue. I remember getting in her car and her taking me down to the city morgue. I think it took us a while to find the place. Yet, I had to go and get my son, Mack. He needed me and he was all alone. I felt so helpless, so lost. I never want to feel that way ever again. I kept calling Jesus and asking for his mercy. I imagine that is how He felt when He was all alone on the cross bearing our sins. I do not even remember where everyone was or where they went. For that matter, I do not even remember how Sandy got there. She told me, I think.

Sandy comforted me and did something that no one else had done yet. She took hold of my hands and she started to pray. Sandy prayed to the Father and the Son for His grace and mercy upon our family. She asked the Lord to reveal and catch Mack's murderer and bring him to justice no matter who it might be. Looking back, I wonder did she know at that point that it was her nephew? She asked that we would be shielded so the pain and sorrow would not destroy us but make us strong. Sandy and I cried holding on to each other. She waited patiently while uncontrollable sobs tore from my throat and my body trembled with hurt, sorrow, and fear. When Sandy and I arrived at the morgue, I rang the bell and picked up the speaker-phone to talk to the man inside; or maybe it was just an intercom I spoke over. I just remember hearing his voice. He inquired as to why I was there and how he could help me. It was around midnight. I could not begin to recall what happened to those hours in between the time I arrived at the scene of the crime and arriving at the morgue. It was like a dream or rather a nightmare. I informed the man that I needed to see my son to identify his body. I had to give him the street where the shooting occurred as well as the name of the victim. When the man checked the information I had given him, he told me that I would not be able to see the body because it was in no condition to be viewed. He first asked me if I knew that there had been a wound to his face and I answered that I had heard it had been. He told me that there was a wound to his face and that there was not much to work with.

I thought about Mack's handsome face. I started to cry, and shake and I heard him say that he would try to get it prepared and to come by tomorrow morning to see him. I guess he was trying to comfort me by withholding some of the cold, hard facts about Mack's death. I later remember him confirming that he had been shot three times when in actuality it was eight times according to the autopsy. Looking back, I do appreciate what he was trying to do. I would imagine that in his line of work, he has had to hear many screams, sobs and sounds of torment. However, sometimes even though the truth may hurt, it is better to tell it. As I sat in Sandy's car and relayed the information to her that the man at the morgue relayed to me; reality set in and my heart crumbled. Everyone was meeting up at Kay's house. People were coming, going, crying, drinking, and trying to be supportive. However, I was not there. My body was there but my mind was in the care of Jesus Christ, the Righteous. I felt calm but removed from the circumstances around me.

Where was Pete? My aunt came in from Chicago early the next morning and took charge of ministering to our needs. I thank and praise God for her. Nevertheless, all the events that followed from the time I saw my daughter Lanie's face up through Mack's home going service, were muted and some still are. People started to speculate as to who did it and conclusions were made based on pure adrenaline and little facts.

~The Devil Had To Get Permission!~

That night, as I lay in one of the beds at Kay's house, I was torn between leaning on the Lord and giving in to my grief. If I gave in to my grief, at the moment, I felt like I wanted and was going to die. I guess I finally fell off to sleep. However, I woke up screaming and kicking; and Lanie came in and we cried and rocked each other for comfort. The next morning my aunt cooked a marvelous breakfast and she insisted that we all eat something. Pete still talks about how good her cooking was. He calls it supernatural cooking! I always knew that Mack was special because so many people cared for him. He had a thing for taking up with the underdogs. Mack never seemed to put people down because of who they were or what they did. He was a real peacemaker, which is what I was told he was doing that caused his death. It appeared that he was helping a relative to move out because her next-door neighbors were giving her family the flux. The teens from both houses started to bicker, argue and fight each other which is why they called him down.

Mack came down, yelled at the teens, and put a little fear verbally into them and the teens retreated into the house I was told. In the interim, someone threw a bottle (not Mack) at the door of the house where he was reprimanding the teens. Someone from the house called someone else and they came in three cars with guns looking to kill. When the murderer came on Mack's property looking for him, I was told that Mack tried to reason with him. Mack tried to tell him that it was only a couple of teens and he had straightened it out without putting his hands on anyone, mind you. However, Satan had already sought with the Lord to take Mack's life. Mack's job on this earth apparently was over. There is nothing done that the Lord does not allow. Satan has to get permission from God to harm anyone.

Lanie was right there with Mack and tried to encourage him to run. Lanie said she told Mack that the man was coming with a gun and that bullets had no names. However, Mack replied “these bullets have names on them.” Did he possibly know somehow that he was going to die? Lanie said that it seemed as though the killer’s gun had jammed. When it appeared to Lanie that Mack was not going to move, she grabbed his arm and pulled him up off the porch and began running with him toward the back of the house in the field. Mack was hit with multiple gunshots. Mack fell to the ground and began to crawl and Satan walked him down and shot him in the head and face another four times. Yes, Satan had a mission and he had to complete it.

I must leave off the rest of the details. I still cannot report the gory facts in detail. Maybe one day, I will be able to, but it is not this day.

I just remembered that Lanie said the day before Mack had said something to the effect that he wanted her and Gina to stay close because he was not going to always be around. Lanie said she felt a little unsettled and did not want to talk about it. So Mack smoothed the subject over by saying that he would probably live to be at least 80 something. He knew that Lanie would have never accepted the fact that he was getting ready to leave her. Gina had said that Mack did not even want to leave out of the house at all that day. He had just gotten a new game and said he was going to play it. Gina and Lanie had said Mack did not even want to smoke a cigarette. Do you know that according to his autopsy, Mack had no alcohol or drugs in his system?

People told me that I started to sing at Mack's Home Going; and, it was so anointed that the young man who was originally singing the song gave me his microphone. Praise God. However, the memory of that at best is minimal. I do remember lots and lots of faces, most of which still remain a blur to me. There was nothing real about anything that was going on around me. I remember reading the signatures in his memorial book and reading cards thinking; was this person there, was that person there, I do not remember this one or that one being there.

CHAPTER 5} CHANGED LIVES FOREVER

~Sons!~

The day after Mack died, we went back to the morgue. It was Pete, Sr., Pete, and one of Pete, Sr.'s nieces and me. We wanted to identify the body. I mean, after all, that would seal the doubt in my mind and in my heart. Would it not? I mean, somewhere inside of me I had a small amount of hope that the body was not really Mack's. Yet, still I was not prepared for what I saw and even less, for what I did not see. They had us to fill out some papers and then ushered us into a room. The room had a few chairs and what appeared to be a TV or computer screen. There may have been a couple of tables in the room also. After a while, the attendant entered the room with (I want to say disc or video, I cannot recall which) something, which he put into the computer. He scrolled through some information and then pulled a picture up on the screen. He turned to us and asked, "Is this him, is this your son"?

I stared at the screen in front of me. I thought maybe if I get a little closer, I would be able to see a little better. I leaned closer toward the screen and what I saw caused me to fall on the floor and cry in agony. On the screen was a satin cloth covering everything except one corner of a mustache, a small part of a mouth and a small piece of a chin. When I say small, I mean small as in less than half. I barely could tell what I was looking at. The attendant replied that this was all he could show us. I later learned that Mack's head had been blown away and that his brains and fluids had drained out.

It took me two years before I could actually write that down. As much as it hurt, I knew that the small amount of facial area I was viewing belonged to Mack, my son. Mack's father Pete, Sr., Pete and my niece once again went back to the morgue the following day. They were hoping to see a little more of Mack for a more positive identification. However, they were not able to see much more than they had already seen except to identify his clothing. One thing for sure, we were all in agreement that what part we saw belonged to Mack. How is it possible to go on breathing for another second? All things are possible with God. Jesus is our peace, our perfect peace.

A few days after my son's death, they arrested a suspect. Yet, for some reason there was no elation in my heart. I did not feel the urge to celebrate. I did not feel any hatred or dark thoughts. Sometimes I felt guilty because I was not thinking of anger or seeking revenge. In reality, I felt more sorrow for the young man they had arrested. I had come to realize that I was a new creature in Christ and that our minds become renewed. We put away the old man and kill the flesh each day. Before I was saved, I would have wished this young man dead and might have done something stupid to help him along. Now I was determined to pray for this young man and forgive him as Christ forgave me. I recall thinking that if he were found guilty, his mother would loose a son as I lost a son.

On the day of this young man's arraignment, there was a lot of tension and animosity in the courtroom. His family members displayed no compassion for us. Neither did they seem to care that we had lost a loved one to such tragic circumstances. They just glared at us with disdain because their loved one was in a hot spot. I was to find out why, seven months later. As we sat there waiting, heated comments were spat around the courtroom, Pete stood and spoke by the spirit of the Lord and asked for peace. Fortunately, everyone seemed to have listened and the courtroom calmed down. The court made a determination that there was enough evidence to bind the young man over for trial. They were charging him with premeditated first-degree murder. I was grateful that justice was to be served.

I would let you in on a secret right here. However, I do not want to spoil the surprise. Was he sorry for what he had done?

• • •

Our lives had been changed forever and only God knew what we would do next. Each one of us had to try to deal with the pain of losing their child, grandchild, brother, husband, father, uncle, nephew, cousin, and friend. Mack was something in all our lives. I went on with my life by praying, going to church and staying close to Jesus. I found scriptures in the Bible plus others gave me scriptures that I found strength and comfort in. I believed that God, who knew all things, would have His revenge on the accused murderer and anyone else who was involved either directly or indirectly.

~July, July, Oh July!~

On July 27, Mack's remains were interred, better known as cremated. If that was not the right thing to do then I ask God to forgive us all because we were ignorant. I still do not know if it is right or wrong to burn a body rather than bury it. Family members expressed that Mack would have wanted to be cremated and have his ashes thrown out over the river. Mack's home going service was held on July 29. Imagine that!

I knew I needed to keep a handle on the idea of death and its real meaning. I will tell you why. I have five grandchildren as well as myself, who celebrate birthdays in the month of July. One of their birthdays is the day before Mack's death and another one's birthday is the day after Mack's death. How were we going to fit a death in amongst all that celebration? God always answers our questions and/or prayers. One of the evangelist from church told me to read II Corinthians 5:6-8. *"Therefore we are always confident, knowing that whilst we are at home in the body we are absent from the Lord. (For we walk by faith, not by sight")* We are confident I say, and willing rather to be absent from the body, and to be present with the Lord." When I read these scriptures, I had a new revelation. My son, Mack was no longer in his tabernacle, but instead was present with the Lord. How satisfying to know that. I had heard it read that Jesus died that we may live. I could just feel my faith in the Lord growing to a higher level each day.

At first, I had difficulty figuring out what to do with myself. I knew something was missing and I was hoping that my belief and faith in the Lord Jesus would be enough. He said in His word that His grace is sufficient for thee. His strength is in our weakness. Therefore, I knew that eventually everything would work out. In my studies, I learned that *"many are the afflictions of the righteous, but the Lord delivers us out from them all."* Psalm 34:19 I knew my afflictions were just beginning.

CHAPTER 6} IF A HEART CAN CRY

~Twin "A" And Twin "B"~

We had been at the hospital all day. They had tried to stop Lanie's labor but it did not appear to be working. We had actually arrived the night before and were still there. Lanie was approximately five months into her pregnancy. We had just learned the startling fact from her ultra sound that she was not having just one baby, but two instead. We also were told that one baby might be in trouble. Somehow, the baby had broken away from the wall of the placenta and was not receiving proper nourishment. I only know I needed to pray. I prayed for Lanie and I prayed for the babies. We had just suffered a tragedy a month ago and I did not welcome any more bad news. Yet, I knew in my spirit that God had to have his way and whatever happened in this hospital would be part of his perfect plan for our lives. Would my Lanie feel the same way? I called on other members of the family and friends from church, plus the pastor for special prayers.

On August 29, 2003, exactly one month after Mack's Home Going service, Lanie gave birth to two baby girls. They were very small, weighing 1 lb. 13 oz. and 2 lbs. and 3 oz. They were beautiful and fully developed on the outside. Unfortunately, being premature they had things going on in the inside, especially Twin "A." Her organs, specifically her kidneys had not developed enough to sustain her life. I could only comfort Lanie by telling her that God knows what is best for all of us. I gently reminded her that it was totally in His hands.

Many people were showing their concerns and stopped by to say a prayer for Twin "A," as well as Twin "B." Even the doctor and nurses along with the chaplain were saying prayers. However, on September 1, 2003, the Lord Jesus carried the spirit of little Twin "A" in His bosom to be with Him in heaven. Lanie held the baby in her arms as she took her last breath while I stood by watching in silence. Lanie was devastated and brokenhearted. The pain started in my bones and crept up into my heart. Since this was the first time I had witnessed a death, I was astonished when the nurse put Twin "A" in the bed with Twin "B." She laid them side-by-side and said she was letting Twin "B" say good-bye to her sister, Twin "A." She took pictures of them lying together and Lanie asked if she could have one. The nurse gave her a few of the pictures. As God is my witness, Twin "B" had a tear in one eye. Maybe she knew the life she had grown with and been connected with over the past five months was no longer present.

I recall how agitated Lanie and I both were when the woman doctor had told us the news that Twin "A" would probably not live. I am sure she has seen many, many deaths of newborn babies. I imagine in the beginning it probably hurt her to see little babies slip away. How do you shield yourself from so much pain? Nevertheless, I did not care for the urgency in her voice when she was trying to convince Lanie to sign papers to have Twin "A's" body donated to the University for study. She related that the study would help them in learning what problems and concerns cause death in premature babies. However, who can concentrate on signing papers to give away a child who you do not want to die in the first place. Nevertheless, when all attempts to save the baby had failed, Lanie signed her daughter over to be studied in hopes that many other babies would be saved.

Lanie was grieving badly and had to leave out. Soon after she left, they brought the baby to the family waiting room so that we could say our final good-byes. I was there along with the baby's grandfather, Pete, Sr. We sat watching for a while and then he left out. I picked the baby up and stared at her precious little face. The tiny body was still warm. However, as I sat there and watched I could see death taking away all signs of life from the little body. I kissed her little cheek and told her how much I loved her. I whispered to her that she would now be with her Uncle Mack who had fallen asleep last month and that he would take care of her. Then I laid her back down in her crib and took my leave. All the while, I was in awe because I had never seen death up so close. Without the spirit of the living God inside of our bodies, we dry up and become as dust.

There were so many thoughts going through my head at that moment. I knew God was real but why was he not hearing our prayers? I even thought we were being punished for something. Those are the type of thoughts that the enemy will plant in your spirit to try to turn you against God. The enemy tries to make you think God does not love you. However, no matter what I thought, there were one or more scriptures to support my belief and dispel my fears. When I felt as though God did not know or care that my heart was broken not once but twice in a little over thirty days, I was given the following scripture by a fellow saint: "The Lord is nigh unto them that are of a broken heart; and saves such as be of a contrite spirit." Psalms 34:18 I truly needed to read that. My soul drank the words up as a thirsty nomad lost in the desert; right about now my spirit was indeed crushed.

I kept thinking of what I could say to my hurt and desolate child. I wanted Lanie to love the Lord not hate or blame Him. I knew she did not understand what was happening in our lives and I was just coming into the understanding myself. King Solomon who possessed more wisdom than anyone before him as well as anyone after him said, "To everything there is a season and a time to every purpose under the heaven." I was beginning to believe that this was our season. Did King Solomon not also say that there is a time to be born and a time to die? I also read that God has no respect of person. That means that He thinks of us all as equals. What happens to one person can certainly happen to the next. Like most people though, we never thought these things would happen to us. Some part of me wanted to be angry with someone or blame someone. After all, how did Lanie's doctor not know she was having twins?

I am not sure how much time went by before Lanie returned. I just knew I was happy to see her come back. Although my heart was heavy, there was still one very important fact we had to consider. There was still one baby very much alive, Twin "B." Lanie came back because she knew all her hope was not gone but lay in the bed opposite where Twin "A' had lain not long ago. I was never more proud of Lanie as I was at that moment. I watched her as she sat beside Twin "B" and I knew in my heart that Twin "B" was going to live and be healthy. What a great God we serve!

~Count It All Joy!~

I was so tired, having slept very little over the past three to four days. I also felt weary and a little afraid of what the future held for my family and me. I knew that Satan had a plan to destroy our family structure as was his plans for all families that had the love of God in them. I had been praying so much. I knew that some power or force was holding me and keeping me from falling apart. Although we were going through some trying times, I knew that somewhere, someone was going through worse. I was still having trouble understanding why or how a person could bear so much pain. Why does God allow us to suffer? God loves us for sure. That is why He gave His only begotten son to die for our sins so that we may live for eternity. When our faith is tried, it builds up patience. James, who was the brother of Jesus said, "Count it all joy when we fall into various trials." I think that means that without trials and tribulations, there would be nothing to test our faith or our trust in God. I firmly believe the Lord does not burden us with more pressures or blessings than we can bear. I told you earlier that, however I may be thinking or feeling, God speaks to me through one or more scriptures. When God speaks to us, it is usually through someone, something written or something heard. I have yet to literally hear His voice. I imagine that as much as I love the Lord, I would be frightened if He started to speak to me aloud.

• • •

"**A time to** kill and a time to heal." Yes, this was our time to heal. No one in the family ever received any professional counseling. Even now, I vaguely wonder why. Church members acted as though they were afraid to mention Mack's death or little Twin "A." The pastor never said much. He did mention once to the congregation that he admired my tenacity in that I did not appear to let the death of my son get the best of me emotionally. I am glad they could not see my pillow at night. I am glad that I had the Lord Jesus to lean on. I was holding so firmly to that belief that I was afraid to openly mourn or show grief. I thought that God would be upset because He felt I did not trust Him to get me through these tragedies. This is the beauty of the scriptures. *"Blessed are they that mourn for they shall be comforted."* Matthew 5:4 It is evident that God knew we were destined to go through trying times. No wonder He instructed the men of God led by the Holy Ghost, to write the wonderful scriptures of His Word, the Bible. Only when I allowed myself to grieve did I start to heal.

I was cleaning my house one day and I happened to look up at my son, Mack's picture. I had a poster size picture of him on a shelf in the dining room. His box of ashes sat in a gift bag in front of the picture poster. We had not bought an urn for the ashes because we were undecided whether we were going to keep them or scatter them over the river. We were waiting for his murderer to be tried and convicted. At any rate, I was staring at his picture when I opened my mouth and began to sing, "My son, I love you" when I got half into the song, I ran and got paper and a pen. I knew the Holy Spirit was giving me a song and I had to write it down. I am going to have the song recorded one day. It really touched my heart. I began to thank God for giving me a song. For *"in everything give thanks: for this is the will of God in Christ Jesus concerning you"* (1 Thessalonians 5:18).

Yes, I grieved. I let it out. I cried daily. I thanked the Lord for letting me know that it was okay to grieve. I missed Mack and did not think it possible to be normal again. After all, my world consisted of my four children and their children. Have you ever been eager to put a puzzle together? Just when you think you are done, after hours or maybe days of trying to get it done, you find that the very last piece is missing. Well that is how I felt. I have a beautiful family, a little dysfunctional; yet still beautiful. However, a piece is missing and now the family is incomplete. I know that in time, God will replicate the perfect piece to fit in the puzzle. For when He begins a perfect work in us, He sees it to completion. With God, where there is a beginning, there is ultimately an end.

~Little Twin "B"~

Little Twin "B." She was a beautiful little girl. Lanie would go to the hospital each day. In the beginning, after Twin "A" fell asleep, she stayed at the hospital overnight. Sometimes I would go and sit with Twin "B" and give her a chance to go home to be with her other children. Lanie started the "Kangaroo" program with Twin "B." They would undress the baby and Lanie would put her beneath her blouse, right next to her skin. What a wonderful program. Twin "B" just flourished under the program. She gave her baby girl the fabric of what holds the world together. *"For God so loved the world, that He gave His only begotten Son..."* John 3:16 That son is Jesus. After a couple of months in the hospital, Twin "B" was finally able to come home where she would be showered with love and affection from her mother, brothers, sisters, and me. She was doing so well and she had only one obstacle. She had to use an oxygen tank. This was only for a while to make sure her little lungs were good and strong. Eventually, she was taken off the oxygen. Twin "B" started growing and responding like any full term baby. She was a little small for her age, but that just made it a little more fun to be with her. Sometimes, we mothers feel our children grow up too fast. Being small just enhanced her baby character even more.

I really poured myself into Twin "B." Her mother, Lanie was away often during the day and with the other children at school all day, it was just Twin "B" and I. Caring for her gave me a sense of purpose again as well as helped me to keep from thinking of my son, Mack so much. I felt that Jesus had sent Twin "B" to comfort me and to somehow compensate for the loss of Mack. It had been well over three months since his death.

While watching Twin "B" during the day, I also designed and built my very own website. It was designed to reach out to parents, relatives and friends of victims of gun violence. "VOGV" which stands for Victims of Gun Violence is the name that I had given my website. I came up with the idea because people came over and phoned in their condolences and concerns. This all happened right after Mack was murdered. However, after what seemed a short period, the people stopped coming by and the calls stopped coming in. I truly had no one to share my experience with or to give me encouragement. There are times when you need to reach out to another human being and just talk or hear an uplifting word.

My site was designed so people could voice their opinions regarding their loved ones and relay their stories. I also listed names of government agencies, grief counselors and other helpful sites where they obtain information needed to help through their grief. One of my favorite areas to visit on the site was the "Poetry" section. There were poems of love, family and inspiration. I pray that by the time this story is published, VOGV is up, running on full and flourishing. We become victims also when one of our family members has been taken away from us at the hands of a murderer or murderess for that matter.

CHAPTER 7} GOD'S EYES ARE EVERYWHERE!

~Will The Real Murderer Please Stand Up?~

I continued to grow spiritually in the Lord. I went to Bible classes, worship services and fellow-shipped with other saints of God. Twin "B" was getting stronger and more beautiful each day. Then one day, we received a phone call from a detective who was working on Mack's murder case. It was relayed to us that two people had come into the precinct, signed affidavits stating that the accused man they had in jail was innocent; and, that a judge had signed an order for his immediate release. They had named another man as the suspect and the order for an arrest warrant was issued. (It was my thought that the other party accused would have to be in custody before allowing an accused murderer to go free without a trial. Do you remember that I said people were sitting around speculating what happened? In addition, do you remember that I said my daughter; Lanie was with

Mack when he was shot? Well Lanie saw the assailant. She literally stared him in the face.

That night, the name of one of the men who was at the scene of the crime was mentioned in conversation. It was thrown out there that he was the one who probably shot Mack. It was said that earlier that day, Mack had stated that this guy was one of the last people he wanted to see. Ironic isn't it? He might have been one of the last people my precious Mack did in fact see. It seems this guy had an unsavory reputation and everyone there latched on to his name like a fish on worm bait.

Lanie was in shock and everyone was saying "I bet it was him, wasn't it Lanie?" I understand that they even went as far as to get a visual aid of this guy and watched it. Lanie, however, did not.

After a day or so of questioning from the police, Lanie agreed that it was indeed this particular fellow that everyone else told her it probably was. Even the police thought that it was this guy. Sitting in the back of the police car giving her statement, I am positive that Lanie was still in shock.

Incidentally, this guy was an up and coming "gangster" rap artist, who in his video shot someone in his head with an "AK47." He stated that he never leaved home without his "AK." Lanie picked him out of a line up from a picture on a CD cover that had been shown to her. Her state of mind during this period was so fragile and she was leaning on all of us for support. I must admit; everyone wanted someone to be responsible for Mack's death.

Now, here they are on the phone, the detectives, telling us that they have issued an arrest warrant for a different person. How can that be possible? However, as I look back, it was quite possible. I remember Lanie asking once, what happens if you identify the wrong person? At the time, I replied that God knows who did it and if the guy in jail did not do it, he would be set free. I also remember that shortly after the rapper was arrested, two of his people came to see me.

One was the rapper's brother and the other, a big guy, was the brother of the second guy accused of the murder. The fact that the shooter was the big guy's brother did not come out until later. They came to my church one Sunday and waited until service was over to talk with me. They came to ask me if I would talk to Lanie and ask her to look at another picture. They said they we sure that if she saw this picture, she would recognize the guy in the picture as the real assailant. They told me that they knew for a fact that this other guy was the one who shot Mack and that they would hog tie him and bring him into the police station if Lanie would identify him.

~Uncle, Cousin, Nephew and #6~

Now would be the perfect time to tell you a little more about the big guy who I later found out is the brother of the shooter. Pete has a child by one of his female cousins and Lanie has a child by one of his male cousins. They both happen to be Sandy's children. Pete and his baby's mother used to live with Sandy and that is how he got to know the big guy. Pete and Mack even went to that big music festival down in Atlanta together with the big guy. The rapper might have gone too because he and the big guy have a rap group together. So, when the big guy came to my church and embraced me and told me how sorry he was, I truly believed him. He told me that if he had known it was Mack that the shooting would never have occurred.

Should it have made a difference whether it was Mack or some other poor man? I think not. However, he claimed that he had no idea it was Mack because he liked Mack.

Now, in hindsight, I wonder why were they so positive that the big guy's brother did it? Could they have been right there on the scene? Why did they not do something? Could they have grabbed the guy or something? I did, in fact, mention it to Lanie as well as the acting officers on the case that they had been to see me. Lanie was afraid for me that they knew where to find me. She felt that they wanted to kill all our family.

Anyway, the officers said they were sure they had the right person, which was the rapper. They sure did not give much thought that one of the rapper's family members had actually come in contact with me after they were told not to have any contact with our family. Eventually, the officers (probably after being pressured by the rapper's family) did come to our house begrudgingly to show Lanie some pictures.

• • •

Number Six. Lanie stared at number six. It was as though she wanted to say that it was number six. However, what she said was that number six looked familiar. She repeated that there was something very familiar about him. She said something else to the detectives. I do not remember the whole conversation. However, I do remember hearing them say rather "matter of fact" that they were sure they already had the right man. It appeared as though one of them or maybe both of them had something personal against the rapper that they had in jail. They also stated that the rapper probably paid the two witnesses to come in and point the finger at the big guy's brother. (Funny how that is the same theory the defense attorney used.)

They left and Lanie did not push the issue that number six looked familiar. She knew in her heart that he was in fact the man who killed her brother. Maybe she was afraid to speak up or afraid that the police would be angry with her and charge her with perjury or some other charge. They would have had trouble making the charge stick.

Lanie clearly needed to be under a doctor's care. She was walking and talking but her spirit was all but dead. I do not know for sure though. I cannot tell Lanie's story for her. That would be a whole other book. I do know that I also knew that number six was the real assailant by the haunted look in my Lanie's eyes. I tried to talk Lanie into seeing a doctor also. She was afraid to go anywhere near a hospital. All she could think of is what she saw on the ground when her brother got shot with eight bullets.

Eventually, they did issue an arrest warrant for number six. It appears that the affidavits signed against him were his own mother and his brother, the big guy. They were the ones to turn him in. This is how I found out the big guy was the shooter's brother. He said he saw his brother shoot Mack and his mother said that he told her he had shot and killed a man. It was enough to convince the judge to release the rapper from jail. He was released from jail not long after midnight after being in jail over five months or more.

Did the detectives call our family to tell us the rapper had been released? No, we heard it broadcasted on the radio. It seems the rapper was being interviewed and a big celebration was going on in his behalf.

~Run, Daddy, Run!~

So many places that Lanie went reminded her of when she and Mack had been in those places. Her heart seemed to keep breaking more each time she would pass by a familiar street or see one of their mutual friends. I know; I could feel it too. She told me she felt she could not make it any more. Lanie said she needed Mack back in her life and she was missing him too much. I knew all too well how she felt. I reassured her that Mack would not want her to be as sad as she was and that he would want her to go on with her life. However, one day Lanie came to me and asked how would I like or feel about moving out-of-town. I said fine. I did not feel as though Detroit had anything left to offer me either.

Moving sounded like a breath of fresh air. I prayed about it and waited for the Lord to tell me if I should go or stay. Jesus was the head and leader of my life. We had decided to move to Florida. Pete was living there already and we were to join him.

Oh yes, I forgot to tell you that Pete had left Detroit. It was just hard for us to enjoy anything without Mack. Our first Thanksgiving without him was just a day everyone went through the motions. You could feel there was no real joy and we all were trying real hard to make the occasion joyous. It is not that we were not thankful for our lives and family that was present. However, that piece of the puzzle was just missing and missed. I had to keep praying and asking God to give me strength in the name of His son, Jesus.

• • •

You know, it seems that I keep remembering things. I am glad memories are coming back. After my shock of losing my son, I guess parts of my memory were shorted out. I also remember that two of Mack's children saw his killer. One said he ran in the yard and pointed the gun at her and her friends and told them to move (using the female dog word) and she ran next door to her house. The house next door had a closed in front porch and they ran inside on the porch.

The other child hid behind the garbage can and said she witnessed the whole event. She gave some very accurate details of what she had seen. The killer walked right past her. Although I have left off the gory details involving Mack's death, there are at least three things that stick out. I should point out that they are verbal incidents because there are some visual details that were told to me that I do not imagine I will ever forget.

Anyway, one is after the assailant shot Mack, Lanie said she fell on her knees in front of him screaming out "Why? Why?" Another is when the daughter who hid behind the garbage can told Pete that she saw the devil when he walked up on her daddy and finished him off.

When this same daughter related to us that she said to her dad (which happens to be the last words she would ever speak to him) "Run, Daddy, Run."

Yes, right here it still hurts even after a couple of years have gone by. I know I have to be standing in the shadow of the Almighty God. I know I have to be covered in his feathers or else I would be crazy, in prison, on drugs or alcohol or dead.

CHAPTER 8} THE EXODUS

~Bragging Rights?~

Thanks be to God for His grace and mercy. I have been able to pick up my life and keep going. Do not get me wrong now. It was not always easy going even with having faith. For instance, we heard a rumor that the rapper, after he had been released from jail, was bragging around town. He reportedly said that he had, in fact, put a contract out on Mack's life. He was supposedly angry and upset that Mack had the audacity to discipline his teen-aged children. It was told to us that the teens that were part of the initial incident might have been the rappers.

The rumor hurt us to the core and we were definitely angry upon hearing it. There was talk of retaliation by some family members as well as by some friends. Yet, I relayed to them we cannot let the anger control us. *"Be ye angry, and sin not: let not the sun go down upon your wrath: Neither give place to the devil"* (Ephesians 4:26-27).

When you are walking with the Lord, it is always about exercising your faith. Anger can eat you up inside like a cancer. It can cause sickness and disease along with bitterness. That is why you have to control it and not let it control you. I had decided to forgive the rapper in the love of Christ and leave him in the hands of the Lord.

We decided to have a yard sale to make some extra money. Lanie and I could not afford to take our furniture with us. We were going to sell whatever we could and then give the rest away.

When I first moved into the house that we were now moving out of, we had basically nothing except a couple of mattresses and our clothes. How had we accumulated enough to furnish a four-bedroom house with what Lanie was getting for her baby and my unemployment income? *"...yet have I not seen the righteous forsaken nor his seed begging bread"* (Psalm 37:25).

We had made several different arrangements as to where we would stay when we got to Florida. However, obstacles were coming up to try and block our exodus out of Egypt, which was Detroit, and into what we thought would be the land of milk and honey, Florida. Income was all of a sudden a problem plus we did not sell a lot of items during the garage sale. At one point, it was decided that I would travel with Lanie's two older daughters and she would come down later with her son and the baby girl. She was going to stay and try to sell more items and also wait for her last check.

For a moment, just for a moment, I started not to go but my spirit was tugging for me to go ahead. I could hardly wait to get away from Detroit. I said I would stretch out on my faith and the Lord would provide for us. It appears I have acquired a lot more nerves since I have been saved.

~The Departure!~

Finally, the day came for our departure. I went over the facts in my mind. Our tickets were paid for; we were going to be living with a relative, and I only had $50 dollars in my purse. We had searched over the Internet for an apartment or a house but things did not work out to our advantage. At best, after we both got there jobs were a must! Shay had told Pete to tell me that once I got down there, I could probably work with her at a hotel she was working at.

The girls and I loaded up on the Bus. Looking back, Jesus was always helping to make sure we were cared for and protected. Our bus was scheduled to depart at 6:00 a.m. My daughter, Kay, was designated to pick me up and take us to the station. For some reason, she was late. I tried to keep calm because the worse case scenario is that; we could catch a later bus. When we arrived at the station I had to get the tickets and check our bags. However, because we were running late, I only had time to get the tickets and since the baggage handler was checking luggage at the front of the bus, I rolled mine over to be checked as well. I had been informed that you could have two pieces of luggage per person to go underneath the bus and one small piece of luggage per person to go on the bus overhead. There were three of us traveling, which totaled eight pieces of luggage to be checked.

At first, the driver was irritated and said he could not wait for all that luggage to be checked. I said a quiet prayer; "Holy Spirit, please help us – take charge of this situation." One of my suitcases, I was informed was extra large and heavy. The baggage checker remarked, "Madam, this is too heavy, you cannot take this one." I just kept on praying. "Okay" he says. "You can take it this time but I hope you know this is costing us an extra $44 dollars."

Thank you, Jesus; Oh Praise God. I do not know what I would have done if I had to take the luggage back. Kay had already left and was probably good and out-of-sight.

I sat back and relaxed in my seat. The girls were settled in their seats across the isle from me. Before long, all three of us were fast asleep.

• • •

As I write this I am reminded of an incident that took place after Mack died. Pete and I were outside talking on the porch. There was the sound of a motorcycle coming towards us. The rider pulled up to the house and stopped. He got off the bike, and taking his helmet off, he grabbed Pete and just held him. If I had not known better, I would say it was Mack holding his brother, Pete.

Everything about the rider said Mack. It was awesome. But after a few minutes, the rider started to look like himself and we recognized one of Mack's best friends, Gabe. Gabe and Mack had known each other during their early adulthood years. They had stayed close and Gabe was devastated that Mack was dead. It was just so spiritual that day and for a strange reason inside of me I was extremely glad to see Gabe and was grateful for his coming by when he did. It felt as though Mack had come in Gabe's body. With God, all things are possible.

• • •

When we awoke, we ate a snack and watched the scenery out of the bus windows. The girls were excited to be going to Florida and were chattering away. It was going to be a long ride with an extended four-hour layover in Atlanta, Georgia. What would we do for four hours? I did not know anyone there to call and since I had never been there before, I did not entertain the thought of roaming around downtown Atlanta with two busy little girls.

When we arrived in Atlanta, I bought the girls and myself a light dinner snack. After all, we would not be leaving there until around 11:35 p.m. and it was only about 7:00 p.m. Good, I thought by that time the girls would be good and sleepy. Once again, something would happen to increase my faith in the Lord Jesus Christ. *"Oh taste and see that he is good: blessed is the man that trusts in Him"* (Psalm 34:8).

~Hang Out With Jesus, He Hung Out for You!~

After we sat down to eat, something was telling me to check on our luggage. I have since learned that that something is none other than the Holy Spirit. The Spirit was saying to me that I needed to get up and go make sure they took my luggage off the bus. I went up to the counter to ask the attendant. She advised me that the baggage would be just outside on the side of the terminal in a tent.

What was I going to do with the girls and all of our personal belongings? I did not want to leave them alone but there was urgency for me to go outside quickly. Okay, five minutes. It should only take a couple of minutes to check on our baggage. I told the girls to sit, eat and not move. I told them not to talk to strangers but if the security officer asked, I was going right outside to check the baggage. I left them reluctantly and went to check the tent for our belongings. When I got to the tent, I could not see our luggage inside anywhere. The man in charge told me to ask the driver of the bus I just disembarked from if it was still there.

The bus was loading up and the attendant was putting luggage underneath the bus. "Excuse me, but may I check to see if my luggage is still under here, " I said? His body language already said he did not want to be bothered with me. He gave me a disconcerting look but nevertheless allowed me to look. "There,

there they are," I exclaimed. My heart skipped a beat. Our luggage was getting ready to go to a different city than we were going to without us. When I asked him if he would please take them off for me, he made a strange comment.

I had on a T-shirt that read, "Hang out with Jesus. He hung out for you." Grumpily he replied, "Why don't you get Jesus to do it, you're the one hanging out with him." The remark kind of caught me off guard but I just smiled and said, "I would not have it any other way," all the while praying in my spirit. At least he took them off the bus and sat them on the sidewalk.

By the time I watched the porter put my luggage in the tent, more time had passed by than I wanted to spare. I got back into the building just in time. The girls had gotten up and were running around the terminal, which caught the attention of the security guard. He had them in tow and was headed my way. I began to explain to him the reason I felt it so urgent to check on our luggage. He told me that it was unwise to leave them unattended and I totally agreed. I apologized and promised him I would not do it again. I knew I should not have left them. However, I also relayed to the girls about being responsible. They were disobedient. I asked them specifically not to get up just because of that very reason, that it would draw attention to them.

I was glad to see 11:35 p.m. roll around. Finally, we were on our way and I settled in to take another much needed nap.

~Where Did All The Palm Trees Go?~

As the bus entered Gainesville, I could not shake the dismay I felt. What happened to the beautiful Palm trees and gorgeous scenery I had expected to see? Were we far from the beautiful beaches with lots of sand? There had to be some mistake. After all, Pete had nothing but good things to say and wonderful compliments about this place. That is all he talked about most of the time. However, the bus station we just pulled into was a very small one-stop station. It was surrounded by what looked like a rural area. It had a country, southern look to it. Why had I never thought of Florida as being a southern state? It definitely was confirmed when I heard the different people start to speak. Nevertheless, I like that southern twang and possess a little of it myself being born in Mississippi. Well we are here now and we will have to make the most of it.

When Shay who is my ex-husband's sister, pulled up, I was very happy to see her. We embraced each other in greetings and warm smiles. When Shay came up to Detroit for Mack's home going service that was the first time I had seen her in years. We loaded up her car, piled in amongst the luggage where we could and headed to her dwelling. We chatted all the way, bringing each other up-to-date on our lives since we last met.

Since I did not know that to expect, I was pleasantly surprised when we pulled into a very nice and well-kept apartment complex. Shay pulled into her parking place and I saw her roommate Bonda come out to meet us and to help unload the luggage. In the back of my mind, I wandered how she would have room for us. After the intros were made between Bonda and us, Shay showed the girls and me to the room we would be sharing. She gave up her room for us and I was grateful for that. Pete slept in the living room on the couch.

We settled in, had some dinner and attended a church service later that evening. Shay was a wonderful woman of God. Not only did she offer good spiritual advice but she also offered sound social advice. Shay took me around and showed me all the organizations where I could obtain help for the girls and myself. We were able to secure food and clothing and were signed up for health benefits. With her help,

I got the girls enrolled in a wonderful school and things were moving right along. I even got a job at the same hotel that Shay was working at. Bonda worked at a different one. We all rode together in the mornings and we dropped Bonda off first. Cabinct Lodgc where we worked was a little farther down. Some mornings, Shay allowed me to take the children to school and drop them off. By the time I would get back, we would all be ready to leave for work.

~Recognizing True Saints!~

The Lord was blessing me each and every day. I was even enjoying the southern atmosphere. I attended and worshipped at Shay and Bonda's church, New Israel. Pastor Ewes and his wife were wonderful spirit filled individuals. The church was medium sized but had a small congregation. Yet the Holy Ghost was there whenever we held services. I really loved Pastor and Sister Ewes. They had hearts of gold and also helped the girls and I to be comfortable in our trailer. They gave us a TV, a couple of dressers, clothes for the kids and a few other things. Sister Ewes said the Lord sent me there and it was her job to help me because it was His will. She would try and give me money on a weekly basis to put in church or to have in my pocket. I tried to pay her on occasion but she refused to accept it. She said that as a fellow saint, she was blessed to be able to bless me and my faith rose to another level.

Sister Ewes sold used clothing, shoes and other items from her home and she gave me a nice deal on some clothing that she could have charged a lot more for.

Sister Ewes had a beautiful alto voice and I loved to hear her sing. I often wondered why she never put together a choir. As it was though, I joined their Praise and Worship Team and visited other churches with them. All the while, I was growing in grace. Eventually, the Pastor asked if I would head a youth choir. I accepted and taught them as the Spirit of God led me. Most of the members of the choir were teens with the exception of my granddaughters who were ages eight and six. They loved to sing and praise the Lord also. I felt God was pleased with me because I was doing his will.

I had never heard of dumpster diving. When Shay and I along with the girls, pulled into the lot where the big green dumpster was, I looked in awe. There was a large building resembling a warehouse with doors that open like garage doors sitting off to the side of the lot. It was filled with clothing and there were people sorting through them so that they could dump them in the dumpsters. There were also shopping carts with clothing in them scattered about. The dumpsters were pretty clean as they only contained clothing items. We had fun sorting through and picking out what we wanted. The best part is that they were all free. Shay definitely had her resources.

Most times when I was around Shay and Bonda, I felt welcomed and at peace. I was working everyday and looking forward to finding a place for Lanie, the kids and myself. I truly hoped to find a place before Lanie and the other kids arrived. However there were other times when I felt a little tension in the air. During those times, I prayed even harder to find and be able to afford my own dwelling. I appreciated Shay and Bonda so much for all their help and for opening their home to us. Nevertheless, I did not want to wear out my welcome. It is times like this when Satan gets busy and tries to plant animosity between people.

I looked at several places but there was one apartment complex that was fairly new and absolutely beautiful. Bonda had suggested them and she took me by there to fill out an application. The apartment had three bedrooms and was on the bus line. That meant I could take the bus to work, and Shay and Bonda would not have to go out of their way to pick me up. I claimed the apartment in the name of Jesus and had every reason to believe I would get it. While I waited for the reply to my application, I kept my eyes open for alternatives. One of the alternatives was a trailer park offering rent-to-own one to four bedroom trailers. One of their advertising features was that you only had to pay $500 dollars down to get in and you got one month's rent for free. I had never lived in a trailer park but the ones I saw in passing were exceptionally nice and the grounds were very clean. Yet I wondered what kind of people lived in trailer parks? I was soon to find out.

Working at Cabinet Lodge Hotel was not hard but tedious. Still I rather enjoyed it. I was left alone to clean the rooms and the patrons were very pleasant most times. This was the first time I had experienced this form of work. The manager felt I was moving too slow and had warned me she might have to let me go if I did not pick up my speed. Some days I had as many as 20 rooms and as little as 14. I prayed and expressed my concerns to the Lord. I, if truth were told, needed the job to help get our own living quarters. As I prayed, I knew that I would not be let go because of my speed. All I had to do now was wait for Lanie who would be arriving in about one week. I had been hired in at the hotel for at least three weeks and was working toward getting 30 days into the job.

After my disappointment in not getting the apartment, I had to strengthen my faith. Yes, they had turned me down. "Hope deferred maketh the heart sick…" Proverbs 13:12.

It seemed that someone I used to rent from gave me a bad report, except he was a liar. I not only used to rent from him but I also worked in his office. He was under the demonic spirit of money when I worked for him and although I gave him a 30-day notice that I was moving, he still filed a judgment against me in court. Go figure. *"For the love of money is the root of all evil: which while some coveted after, they have erred from the faith, and pierced themselves though with many sorrows."* I Timothy 6:10

CHAPTER 9} THE ADJUSTMENTS

~Satan, My Children and The Trailer Park!~

I did not understand why Jesus did not allow me to get the apartment but I was not going to question it. I knew there had to be a reason. Everything that happens fits into His plan for His perfect will. I knew that "they that wait upon the Lord shall renew their strength…" I remembered the trailer park advertisement. I had been holding on to it and when Pete mentioned that his friend, Selena suggested we try applying. It was also a good suggestion because she personally knew Mr. Harry who was in charge of the park. I knew the Lord had to be guiding me to go ahead. Lanie had sent some money down to put a deposit on whatever establishment I found for us. Selena volunteered to take me to the trailer park to fill out the application. I had already spoken to Mr. Harry on the phone and he assured me that my daughter and I together would qualify to get into a 3-bedroom trailer. I was excited and could not wait to share my news with Lanie. The trailer was a very nice 3-bedroom, 2-bath Eldora do style home. I had filled out the application ad after viewing the trailer, put a deposit down on it. By the time, Lanie arrived and I got my next paycheck, we would be all set to move in.

Lanie had been making excuses for not leaving Detroit yet. The date she originally was supposed to come, she called saying she could not make it and that she would be down later. Her scheduled arrival, however, was right on time for the move. Unfortunately, our home was not ready when she got to Florida. I was so glad to see her and my grandson. But I was even more thrilled to see Twin "B." She was so pretty yet still a bit small. I could not stop kissing and squeezing her. Every day that I came home from work, I grabbed her up and kissed and hugged her. I had missed her so much. With working each day, going to church at least three times a week and taking care of the girls, it helped to keep my mind of my son, Mack. I was glad Twin "B" was back in my life. I had not seen her in close to a month.

When you are a child of God, you learn to expect Satan to try to attack and sabotage your blessings. There was some type of delay in getting the trailer ready. Lanie had already been there at least a week and the management was assuring us that today it would be ready.

It was becoming quite close with Lanie, her four kids and myself all in one room, Shay and Bonda sharing a room and Pete on the couch. It was just a few too many in a 2-bedroom apartment. It was Friday and I was looking forward to Monday, which was my scheduled day off. I had just gotten off work and was headed to the apartment. It was only Shay and I because Bonda had the day off. When we got to Shay's there was an aura of confusion and tension in the air.

Apparently, Pete and Lanie had been arguing and when I got out of the car, they both were eager to ask me a question. Because I am only telling my story, let us just say the question was something related to Pete's past behavior. In hindsight, I wished I had ignored them and refused to answer. However, I did respond and my response was more in line with whatever Lanie had been saying instead of Pete.

Out of the four of my children, it was usually Pete and Lanie who just could not get along with one another. If they were around each other for more than an hour or so, they would ultimately wind up disagreeing about something. When a mother loves her children, she certainly does not want either of them to fight or get hurt, especially the girls. At any rate, one word led to another. Shay, who favored Pete, already had her continence set against Lanie or so it appeared to me.

We, as Christians, sometimes handle critical situations no better than heathens.

At any rate, Shay started in reprimanding Lanie who was already angry. Lanie had calmed down and leaning on the side of compliancy when Shay made a comment that set Lanie off again. I wished Lanie had been able to accept criticism better. After all Shay was her aunt as well as her elder. Unfortunately, Shay had said something about beating Lanie's behind and Lanie was the type that would fight Goliath if he had approached her. She could have very well been a female David. I tried to tell Pete and Lanie to be quiet, but my voice was lost on the wind. Shay told Lanie she wanted her to leave with that type of attitude.

At that moment, Lanie held up a set of keys and said fine, I was leaving anyway or something to that effect. I was astonished but relieved at the same time. I was caught in the middle of something ugly and only God was going to be able to bring peace into the situation. Shay went into the house and began packing up all of our clothes, including Pete's, and setting them outside on the lawn. She was fired up. I felt sad because we, up to this point, had a wonderful Christian relationship. My disappointment in Lanie and Pete as well, was nothing short of disgusting. Pete was a saint but he reacted to Lanie in the flesh and that allowed Satan to come in and try to tear us all apart.

When demons come to spread disharmony, strife and even violence, they strike at whomever they can reach, usually the weakest link. You have to constantly have your armor on. *"Put on the whole armour of God, that ye may be able to stand the wiles of the devil"* (Ephesians 6:1).

I went into the house to pack the rest of my belongings. Since Lanie had gone to the trailer Park and gotten the keys earlier that day, I was at least glad to not have to worry about where we would stay. However, Shay started in on me and in so many words blamed me for Lanie's behavior. I made a comment to her and she exploded in anger. Well, it was then that I just girded my loins. I refused to keep arguing with her. Pete intervened at the point when he thought she might strike me. She threatened to physically harm me. I had reminded her that in the name of Jesus and all that was holy, her behavior was unacceptable as a Christian woman.

Lanie and Pete left in Selena's car to take the first load of our clothing. We had not rented a trailer or truck because the move was so unexpected. I was left in the yard with the rest of our belongings. Shay and Bonda had stayed in the house. Where their front door was usually open to catch the late spring breeze, it was now closed.

~Hah! Foiled Again Satan! ~

I sat at one of the little white tables in the yard asking the Lord how could things have gone so wrong? This was not how I wanted to leave Shay's house. After what seemed a long time, Selena pulled up with Pete. Lanie and the kids had stayed at the trailer. They got out and helped to put the rest of the items in the car. We had everything loaded and were ready to go. Yet there was something I felt I needed to do before I left. I had gotten in the car but I told Selena that I felt bad about leaving in strife. We both agreed that I should make peace before I left. I knocked on the door and when Bonda answered, I told her I needed to see Shay for a moment. Shay was reluctant to talk to me. I did not wait for any response from her. I grabbed her and hugged her and told her I was sorry. I asked for forgiveness if I offended her in any way. I finished the conversation off with my thanks for everything that she had done for us and told her that if she needed me, she could always come to me. I also thanked Bonda and then I left. I thanked Jesus for giving me strength to do what I had just done.

If Pete had told me what Shay had said about me before I made peace with her it might have taken me a while longer. Apparently, she made a derogatory comment that she could have had her way with me like a man. Shay had to have known better because I have never preferred the opposite sex and thank God for Jesus in my life, never would. I must admit I was pretty fired up but I knew it was just Satan trying to anger me to the point that I would confront Shay about what she said. Hah! Foiled Again Satan. I took it to the Lord instead and was glad I had made my peace.

I was very pleased with the trailer. It was more than enough room for all of us. Even though we had absolutely no furniture, at least we were not on the streets. It was time to take care of business. Life still had to go on. Unfortunately for me, our home was located 2½ miles from the nearest public bus stop. I thought about walking, but I was just not use to Florida's hot, sunny weather yet. Sometimes Lanie and Pete would walk or ride the bikes to the store and they would be so hot and exhausted when they returned. At any rate, it was just a little too far in my opinion to walk. I therefore gave up my job. Because of the recent conflict with Lanie, I knew Shay was not going to pick me up and I did not know anyone else yet, other than Selena. We were going to have enough cash to pay our rent and an ample amount of food provisions each month. Consequently, we were prepared. The trailer was already equipped with a stove and a refrigerator. It also had central air. Yes, God was a wonderful God.

The stove was operated by gas. I was informed that tenants had to order a propane tank that sat in the yard beside the trailer. We had not had the opportunity to order any gas tanks so Lanie decided to go across to our park area and use one of the built-in grills to cook some chicken. The trailer park had its own swimming pool, duck pond, playground area and park area for its residents. It was then that she met Mr. Jerry. He as an elderly white man and appeared to be very friendly. Mr. Jerry always walked around the park with his little dog. He asked Lanie why was she using the park grill. He told her that the ducks usually poop all over them. Lanie had cleaned it before she used it, and informed him that we could not use our stove yet because of our lack of propane.

Mr. Jerry told her he would get us one and have the company bring it out. He said he wanted to make sure that all of us had a way to cook, eat and keep warm when it got cold. Florida gets cold?

True to his word, the man from the gas company came out with the tank and installed it in the yard beside the trailer. I asked him how much it would cost to refill or replace the tank and he told me they ran approximately $200. Who were we that Mr. Jerry would order us a tank and he said we did not owe him anything. I had offered to pay him even though $200 was a little hard to obtain at that moment. Mr. Jerry said absolutely not because he was glad to be able to help someone. Lanie and I were delighted and appreciative. I began to praise and thank God for what he had sent Mr. Jerry to do for us. Even though we were perfect strangers, this man reached out to help us without any ulterior motives. He also let us use his phone a couple of times to call back to Detroit and to the phone company. I found that Floridians were a lot warmer and more compassionate than Detroiters.

Smile Detroiters – you know it is true!

~Life In The Trailer Park!~

Then there was Miss Shirl. Miss Shirl was quite a character. She reminded me of Whoopi the comedienne/actress. She had the dreads and real dark skin. Miss Shirl lived in a 2-bedroom trailer next to us and offered to allow us to use her phone any time we needed. She had one little girl and she and my granddaughters played together almost daily.

Lanie got along pretty good with Miss Shirl and they became friends along with a couple of other people in the trailer park. I was glad she had someone to talk to and especially someone closer to her own age. Although Miss Shirl was closer to my age than to Lanie's, they had more in common with each other than I had with either of them. But Lanie's other friends were more her age. Life was pretty normal at the trailer park. Pastor and Sister Ewes began picking us up for church again. Even Shay finally came around. She even gave us a bed and lots of other things useful for the trailer. She had sent the items by Bonda but at least that was a start. When we finally saw her again, it was almost like old times. I was pleased that Lanie and Shay especially had rekindled their relationship and forgave one another. *"...forgive and ye shall be forgiven"* (Luke 6:37). The spiteful remark Shay relayed to Pete had been thrown into the sea of forgiveness. I never let on that he had told me.

Lanie and the kids enjoyed going to the pool daily. The community in general was friendly and helpful to each other. I was happy and at peace. Peace is something I had not been able to enjoy for a long while. Since Mack had died, I had some restless times. I enjoyed staying in the trailer where it was cool. Florida's heat was so different than any I had felt and I was having an issue getting used to it.

Lanie and Pete had gone back to Detroit. Pete had some business matters to attend to and Lanie went because she had to appear at the arraignment of the guy who killed Mack. I remember the day we found out they had arrested him. Our phone service had been disconnected. I still was not working and income was scarce.

We had made friends with Cora and her daughter when we still lived at Shay's house. Lanie had done Cora's daughter's hair once for a show. Cora's daughter was only 10 years old but had a nice voice and was an up and coming gospel singer. She also was taller than Lanie or me. Anyway, Cora happened to come over to the house one day. We got on the subject of cell phones and as she was explaining her long distance service, I boldly asked if I might use her phone to call Detroit. She said sure and I called Kay to see how all was fairing in the Motor City. Kay and I talked briefly and then said our good byes.

A minute or so after I hung up, Cora's cell phone rang. After looking at her display screen, she handed the phone to me to answer. It was my daughter, Kay again. "Guess what Momma? Daddy called and said they got him – they got the guy who killed my brother and he is talking." I was overcome with thanks to God, relief and joy. Kay said he was arrested for another charge and had given a false name. However, his prints showed who he really was. The police alerted the detectives that they had their man in custody and he could be picked up. Kay said they would let us know when his court date was. When I hung up, Cora and I grabbed each other and started to dance around in the street praising and thanking God for his grace and mercy. "…vengeance is mine, I will repay said the Lord." We both agreed that the Lord had sent Cora by so that I could use her phone to receive the good news.

I would love to have gone but it would have been too expensive for all of us, including purchasing tickets for the children also. I stayed behind and kept all four kids. There were times when I had to really pray for strength concerning the children, that the Lord Jesus would send his ministering angels to help me out. In the meantime, we went back and forth to church worshipping and praising Christ Jesus. One of the things I enjoyed about New Israel was that we were always doing something and fellowshipping with other saints. The mother of the church was an excellent cook and we had dinner on the Sundays that other churches came to fellowship with us.

Lanie had stayed in Detroit about a month. At first, I was beginning to wonder if she was returning at all. When she finally returned, I felt relieved. She could give me a break from the children. I had talked to Lanie while she was still in Detroit and she told me about the arraignment. Lanie just said, "it is him, Mama; he is the one who killed my brother." She said she was sure of it. I felt good. Finally, Lord Jesus, we will see justice rendered.

I had signed up with a charitable organization shortly after I arrived in town, and they came and brought a beautiful dining room table, chairs and a lighted china cabinet. They also bought a wonderful king sized bed along with a couple of small items such as table lamps. I was amazed at how nice our trailer looked.

Neither Lanie nor I had purchased any furniture. We did not have any money for more than rent and utilities. God provided everything that we needed. *"...take no thought for your life, what ye shall eat, or what ye shall drink, nor yet for your body what ye shall put on"* (Matthew 6:25).

~"Sexual Predator and Hurricanes"~

I could not believe it. I pulled his name up and there was a thumbnail picture of his face staring back at me on my computer screen. We had been living in our trailer at least three months and we were just finding out that we were living next door to a "Sexual

Predator." According to the statement information under his picture, he preyed on elderly and handicapped women. Lanie thought Miss Shirl was kidding when she told her about the offender. That is why she had me to look it up on the Internet. God is so good and Jesus reigns. He, the predator, had tried to be friendly with Lanie but she dismissed his advances toward her. Plus he was living with his wife.

One day, before I knew he was an offender, he knocked on my back door with a note for Lanie. I told him that in the name of Jesus, he was not going to bring any confusion to our home by flirting with Lanie and his wife was right next-door. He also knew that Pete was there. I saw him watching Lanie at times so I prayed. *"There shall no evil befall you, neither shall any plaque come near they dwelling. For He shall give his angels charge over thee, to keep you in all your ways"* (Psalm 91:10-11). He never bothered Lane any more and we did not live in fear of him being next door either.

Time really does go by fast. We had been in our trailer for about four months now. The children were in school and the school bus picked them up and dropped them off daily. We had fellowshipped in other cities around the State of Florida. But once we even went all the way to Georgia. We had been on picnics with the Ewes and other church members, including Shay and Bonda. We would all pile up in Sister Ewe's van and she would drive us wherever we had to go. She usually picked the majority of the people up for church and brought them back home again.

We were even there in Florida while Hurricanes Charlie and Frances came through. When Charlie came through, we evacuated the park by order of the management. We went to a motel and spent the night. When we returned the next day everything was fine except for a lot of tree limbs all over the park. However, when Frances came through we decided to ride her out. Frances shook our trailer and doused us with rain for days. It rained for at least three days and the rain was very heavy at times. We just prayed and stayed quiet. When Frances passed and went her way, we still only had a lot of tree limbs all over the grounds afterwards. However, the trailer next door had the top of a tree blocking the exit to their front door. I prayed that all was well inside. Once I saw them open their door, I knew they had faired well.

Now it was September and we were preparing to go back to Detroit for the trial of the man accused of murdering my wonderful son, Mack. We set about trying to figure out what to do with the furniture and all the things we had accumulated in just those four months. We also tried to figure out how we could keep the rent current on our trailer and purchase bus tickets for us all. I prayed. In the end, we left our furniture with Shay. I really wished I did not have to go, but I missed Kay and the rest of my grandchildren. Not to mention the fact that I had to see the man who killed my son, face-to-face.

CHAPTER 10} LORD, LORD, LORD

~What Does A Murderer Look Like?~

We arrived in Michigan the second week of September. Lanie wanted to be there for her birthday, which was the 10th. The trial was to begin on the 29th of September. When he first entered the courtroom, chills went through me, and the first time he looked me in the eyes, I knew he had killed my son. I do not know how I knew but I could feel it deep inside of me. I kept trying to keep my mind objective, although my mind was screaming out "Why, why did you kill my son"? I had to keep reminding myself to let God be in charge.

The Prosecutor, whom I thought started out real strong, began to call witnesses. I was not sure if I would be able to keep it together. I would break into tears sometimes when I heard some gory detail concerning Mack's death. The hardest part for me was hearing his autopsy being read. I would never wish my worse enemy the type of pain that I felt upon hearing what actually happened to his beautiful body. The child that God had given to me that I had raised and loved for the past 30 years. Whew!

We had a chance to talk with the Prosecutor, however, I never really felt that she was 100% sure that she had this case in the bag. She said things like Christian people say. She said vengeance is mine said the Lord or God knows best or justice will be served. She said she prayed over every case before she tried it. I felt confident that the evidence I was hearing would be enough for a conviction. By listening to the defense attorney and his objections, I knew he was trying to plant that shadow of doubt. He kept insinuating that the rapper had paid the two witnesses to sign the affidavits and accuse the defendant of the crime.

I already mentioned that the defendant just happened to be the son of Sandy's blood sister. You remember Sandy, the other grandmother. Just like the serpent told Eve the big lie in the Garden of Eden that cost them to have to move out of Paradise, some child called Sandy's nephew and told him and the rapper a big lie that took my Mack's precious life. That phone call had set the tragic events in motion. Satan saw his opportunity and seized his chance to shed innocent blood.

Sandy and I had decided that being sisters in Christ was more important than hating each other because of our families. Plus the fact that Mack was the uncle to two of her grandchildren, Sandy shared our pains and sorrow. I had even fellowshipped with two of Sandy's sisters and the defendant's grandfather as well. Sandy said she was never really close to her sister and this particular son of hers anyway. Other members of the family did not trust Sandy and preferred to keep their distance. They did not want her to fraternize with us. However, we kept in touch. Since Pete knew the defendant personally he remarked that he could believe the defendant had done it. Pete said the defendant was mean and coldhearted and was also using crack cocaine.

The defense attorney even tried to make the jury believe that Lanie had taken a payment from the rapper. I mean, a sister that loved her brother so much, she begged the defendant to kill her also. She was a train wreck after Mack's death. I think she was forgetting to eat also because she was painfully thin. I wish the defense attorney could feel an ounce of Lanie's pain. I silently wondered if this man knew that his client was guilty. He did kill Mack, didn't he? The witnesses kept coming and different evidence was entered into the records.

The Prosecutor told us the trial would probably last a week. She did tell us that the defense would wear out the fact that Lanie had identified the rapper in the beginning. She was hoping that the jury would understand that she was in shock. In hindsight, The Prosecutor really did not try very hard to persuade them to think that Lanie was in shock. All of our nerves were on edge. We all including the prosecutor had our churches praying for a guilty verdict. Being a saint, I also prayed that not our will but God's will be done.

I sat in the hall and watched the defendant's family as they chatted amongst themselves. Sandy said she would never come to the trial and she did not. However, there were her sisters. There was the sister who signed the affidavit stating that her son told her he had murdered a man; and, that he even told her a few details about Mack's appearance that only someone in close proximity at the time he was shot would know.

The Prosecutor never mentioned the fact about the close proximity. Anyway, this sister sat on the opposite side from the other sisters, one of whom I use to fellowship with in Bible class. She would always greet me with a hug. Although she was not a member of our church, her father was and taught Bible study. Therefore, she would come to be taught by him. In the beginning when they thought it was the rapper, she offered her condolences and said how sorry she was. Now, after finding out her very own nephew was being accused of being a cold-blooded killer, she would not even look at me. The sister who sat opposite them was sitting there with her other son, the big guy. You remember, the one who came to my church to visit me and to tell me he knew who had really shot Mack. I still cannot understand why the Prosecutor never mentioned this fact.

I wonder if one of my grandchildren stuck a gun to my head and robbed me and was breaking in places and stealing, would I say what a good boy or girl they were on a witness stand; especially, if they had gunned down someone in cold blood right in front of their family members. Nevertheless, there she was on the stand attesting to "what a good boy her grandson was." She also stated that he would never do anything like that. Yet the Prosecutor had evidence showing that he had, in fact, been arrested for robbing her at gunpoint, his own grandmother, supposedly to buy drugs. He was never convicted because she, his grandmother, never showed up in court to testify against him. So they, the court, dropped the charges. Why did the Prosecutor have to send the jury out before she could ask the grandmother those questions?

So many questions unanswered.

~The Jury Is Still Out!~

In something as important as a murder trial, if I thought as a prosecutor that I had an ace in the hole; it would have been the fact that one of Mack's daughters had seen, with her own eyes, how her father had been relentlessly gunned down. She even said she knew what he looked like. Yet, they never even bothered to ask. They were worried that it might be too much for her being so young. Will it be too much for anyway? She cannot erase what she saw but I bet it would have been good therapy to help put her father's killer in jail.

Here, we sat in the hall waiting for the jury to come back with a verdict. It was Monday, October 6, 2005 and the jury was out. After about an hour or so, we were called back to the courtroom for the reading of the verdict. Why had they reached a verdict so fast? He must have been found guilty. They certainly had enough evidence against him. We all stood for the reading. "Mr. Foreman have you reached a verdict?"

"We have, your Honor." "How say you?" "…on the count of first degree, premeditated murder, we find the defendant…not guilty!" As the rest of the charges were being read, everything sounded far away. I did not hear that. It must be a mistake. They could not have said "not guilty." I remember saying it had to be a mistake when they said Mack was dead also. I came to myself when I heard Lanie. She screamed and screamed, "but he killed my brother, that was my brother, I loved my brother." They carried Lanie out because the police had the audacity to act as though they wanted to lock her up for her outbursts. I glanced at the defendant and the defense attorney. The look I saw on their faces was one of utter surprise. Was that because they knew he was "guilty?"

A lot has transpired since that day in court. My family has picked up their lives and has moved forward. It is so hard to believe that the pain I felt just five months ago when the jury handed their "not guilty" verdict has subsided to a dull ache. It reminds me of a tiger or panther just watching and waiting to pounce on its prey. I know the pain is pushed down inside of me but like that tiger every now and again, it pounces on me without warning. However, when it does, I go with it and let the tears flow and I just call on Jesus for his tender mercy and comfort. I keep remembering that God bottles our tears in heaven. Isn't that where He is? *"Thou tells my wanderings: put thou my tears into thy bottle: …"* Psalm 56:8

Because the man accused of killing Mack had already been in jail at the time they arrested him for Mack's murder, I was curious to see if he was still in jail. When I called the prosecutor's office, I found out that he had gotten out but had recently been arrested again for larceny and had pled guilty. The advocate gave me a date for his sentencing. Once again, I leaned into my own understanding. I just knew that the judge, after seeing his record of one attempted murder, one first degree murder and countless illegal weapons and robberies, that he would sentence him to prison and he would do something and get even more time. However, he only received, I heard, a three-year probation sentence. Wow!

Who can know the mind of God? *"For my thoughts are not your thoughts, neither are your ways my ways, said the Lord. For as the heavens are higher than the earth, so are my ways higher than your ways, and my thoughts than your thoughts."* Isaiah 55:8-9

I am truly finding out that God has an appointed time for everything. The man who killed Mack has an appointed time to meet with God, the Father and His son Jesus our Lord. I pray that he will be ready. Maybe he will get saved. Can you imagine? But Paul was a persecutor of Christians and killed them on a daily basis. Yet Jesus appeared to him and he became one of the Lord's greatest prophets and disciples. Who can know the mind of God?

• • •

The events I have presented to you took place over the last two years. Talk about trying times and tribulations. I hurt so much, I felt like a human pincushion. I watched so many different family members hurt, crash and burn (not literally) from the pain of Mack and Twin "A's" deaths. When you love someone, if they are hurting, you are hurting also. We, as of this day, are still hurting. I never lost faith though. Even though I do not understand why no one was found guilty or is being held accountable for my son's murder, I have to believe in God's word. *"The Lord hath made all things for himself: yea, even the wicked for the day of evil."* Proverbs 16:4.

~Pete and Paradise!~

While I am typing these last couple of pages, Pete is sitting in prison. Oh yea, I forgot to tell you. Remember Pete was a pistol before he got saved and was on probation for a charge that was a humble. In other words, it was all a lie too. But that is another book.

Anyway, Pete had gotten married and his wife had a baby boy. Apparently, having postpartem depression, she wanted to leave Pete. Pete loved his wife and believing in God did not want her to leave. Yet, she left anyway. During one of the times that Pete and his wife tried to make some type of reconciliation, there was an argument that pursued between her, her parents and Pete and the police was called. Yea, you just about know the rest. Pete probably did something stupid out of desperation but only Pete and his wife knows the real truth. The judge who was over the domestic dispute case gave Pete a 3-year probation sentence. However, when Pete went before the judge to see if he had violated his original probation, in spite of the fact that he was in college, working, had custody of one of his older sons, married, a born again Christian, practicing in ministry and just basically trying to keep his life clean; the judge said Pete violated his probation. He sentenced Pete to 18 months in prison. We are at this very moment trying to get him an early release or get him home on house arrest. Yes, God must have so many bottles of my tears up there in Heaven.

But, guess what? Pete is preaching and ministering even from his prison cell. You go Pete! The Apostles, Paul, Peter and John and a few others all went to prison. God said he would never leave or forsake us. He is even in jail or hell!

I wonder does Pete realize that the same judge who gave the man who murdered his brother a 3-year probation sentence is the same judge who gave him a 3-year probation sentence. Go figure. Who can know the mind of God? *"The righteous perishes, and no man lays it to heart: and merciful men are taken away, none considering that the righteous is taken away from the evil to come. He shall enter into peace: they shall rest in their beds, each one walking in his uprightness."* Isaiah 57:1-2

I know someday we will all find some peace concerning Mack and even Pete for that matter. I do not know how and I do not know when. One thing I do know is that Mack believed in Jesus.

Jesus said unto her:

"I AM THE RESURRECTION, AND THE LIFE; HE THAT BELIEVETH IN ME THOUGH HE WERE DEAD, YET SHALL HE LIVE. AND WHOSOEVER LIVETH AND BELIEVETH IN ME SHALL NEVER DIE. BELIEVEST THOU THIS?" (John 11:25-26)

The End

ABOUT THE AUTHOR

Ethel L. Johnson is a writer, poetess and psalmist. She has been writing for effect since Junior High School where she received a literary award for a short story. The story was about a young girl who had been kidnapped, escaped and found her way back home. Ethel has written and performed a number of songs and poems in school plays, live bands, choirs and praise and worship teams.

Now in her 50's, Ethel had limited her writing to palms and poems and had not considered writing non-fiction until the untimely murder of her oldest son, Isaac. Though grieving, Ethel felt that her story would not only help others through their grief, it was a self-healer for her as well. She has already started on her second non-fiction as well as her book of poetry.

UPCOMING PROJECTS BY ETHEL L. JOHNSON

“Seventy Times Seven”

“A Poem For Such A Time As This”

A Collection of Christian Melodies

www.ingramcontent.com/pod-product-compliance
Lightning Source LLC
LaVergne TN
LVHW091011080826
845145LV00003B/1217